D1161347

FACES OF THE WILDERNESS

HARVEY BROOME

FACES
OF THE
WILDERNESS

PUBLISHED BY
MOUNTAIN PRESS PUBLISHING COMPANY
MISSOULA, MONTANA
IN COOPERATION WITH
THE WILDERNESS SOCIETY
WASHINGTON, D.C.

ALSO BY HARVEY BROOME:

HARVEY BROOME: EARTH MAN
Some Miscellaneous Writings
PUBLISHED POSTHUMOUSLY

FIRST EDITION

TO ANNE

WHO PARTICIPATED IN MOST OF
THESE ADVENTURES, AND WHO
AIDED AND ABETTED ALL OF THEM

FOREWORD

Harvey Broome — a gifted man in the law — was also in the forefront when it came to ecology. In hiking, backpacking, and camping he was a joyous companion. When it came to the preservation of the unique wildness which this continent once knew, he was advocate extraordinary. And when it came to writing about the outdoors and the wilderness, I always rated him along with Henry Thoreau and John Muir.

Deeply appreciative of our wilderness heritage, he was correspondingly sensitive to the problems resulting from man's pervasive compulsion to subdue and exploit the natural environment. He saw and foresaw, as few others of his generation, the price we pay for certain kinds of "progress."

One who reads carefully will detect his deep concern with the ecological problems which have finally reached the consciousness of us all. The book, however, is not an ecologist's catalog nor a reformer's prospectus. The chapters cover hikes and other trips which he and his wife, Anne, took into critical areas that were commanding his attention as President of The Wilderness Society. One gets the environmental message only indirectly; but it is, therefore, even more compelling.

Here is outdoor literature at its best, written by a man who had a discerning eye and who was on a wave length with the life he encountered in the wilds. The reader shares the exhilaration and discomforts of Harvey Broome on these outings and at the end puts down the book feeling that he has been on the seashores, in the deserts, and high in the mountains with a man who loved the earth and honored it for its mystery and beauty.

FACES OF THE WILDERNESS is a partial but revealing autobiography of a dedicated conservationist who put in long and exhausting days to prevent the environmental crisis that promises to overwhelm us.

WILLIAM O. DOUGLAS

INTRODUCTION

Many of the chapters in this volume are accounts of field trips scheduled by the Council of The Wilderness Society in conjunction with its annual meetings. At the outset the meetings were held in Washington, D.C. After he was elected Executive Secretary, the late Howard Zahniser instituted the practice of holding the sessions outside Washington in places of concern to the Society. The first of these was held in 1946, on the edge of the Shenandoah National Park at the foot of Old Rag Mountain. Over the years they have been staged in infinitely more remote and rugged areas, such as the Flat Tops of Colorado, the Salmon River Breaks in Idaho, the Mission Mountains and the Bob Marshall Wilderness in Montana, McKinley Park in Alaska, and the Cloud Peaks of Wyoming.

This book is not intended, however, as a chronology of the field trips of the Council. It is essentially a personal record. Several of the trips were made privately with Anne or with friends. Barring the short opening chapter, each entry has been lifted with but minor editing from my Journals. Each appears in the order of occurrence. Since the entries have extended over nearly a quarter of a century, they are to some extent autobiographical and register a deepening concern over abuses of the land and a parallel concern for the future of man.

Wilderness has many faces. It may be beautiful and friendly, or harsh and trying. We have seen it on rivers and lakes; on deserts; on tundra, snowfields, and glaciers; on beaches and dunes; on mountains and crags; in forests, savannas and meadows; in canyons; and even in temperate jungles and swamps. Sometimes we reached only the fringes of wilderness. Sometimes we were surrounded by it.

The back country of our nation has enormous variety and unspeakable appeal. Each bit of it gets next to you; each experience with it makes you wonder about the rash course of exploitation in our history and the drift toward cultural conformity. The climate, terrain, vegetation, and living creatures found in wilderness have a powerful emotional and intellectual impact. In this volume are my notes of what wilderness has meant to me.

HARVEY BROOME

Knoxville, Tennessee
July 20, 1965

CONTENTS

PHOTOGRAPHS

1

OKEFINOKEE SWAMP
GEORGIA
1938 · 1940

I N SOUTH Georgia, and covering some six hundred thousand acres, is the Okefinokee Swamp. Physically, it is the undrained portion of an uplifted coastal plain, an enormous shallow basin, choked with vegetation and teeming with an extravagant variety of wild things. It is fed by numerous small streams on the north and west; is held back by Trail Ridge on the east; and is drained by the Suwanee River on the southwest. On the southeast, it is reputed to be one of the sources of a second river, the St. Mary's. One authority states that during periods of high water a small overflow finds its way from the swamp into the St. Mary's; another, that the swamp occupies part of the divide between the Atlantic Ocean and the Gulf of Mexico, and that a small portion of its waters drains southward into the headwaters of the St. Mary's. Another writes that in the early nineties when an effort was made to link the Atlantic with the Gulf by means of a canal across the swamp, the project was abandoned when it was discovered that the canal was actually draining the swamp waters into the Suwanee. Available maps usually show one or two tiny tributaries which reach into the swamp and drain to the east. All the authorities agree on one point, that the major drainage is into the Suwanee.

The area lies in the southern coastal plain amid almost limitless reaches of southern pine; and the existence of this lush, moist world of cypresses and Spanish moss, of whooping cranes and alligators, of bonnets and "never-wets," of twisting boat runs, transparent lakes and sweeping "prairies" comes as a surprise to one unfamiliar with the geology of the region. At one time the swamp contained the greatest cypresses in America, huge giants eight feet and more in diameter. Many of these have been removed by logging but much of the best of the swamp has been protected by its very inaccessibility, and is still physically unmolested. Even this central region, however, has long known extensive hunting and fishing.

Three hundred thousand acres of the swamp were set aside in March 1937 into the Okefinokee Wildlife Refuge. All hunting has been stopped, and except for the construction of a stub road to Billy's Lake at the head of the Suwanee River, and the digging of a narrow canal east of Billy's Lake to facilitate patrol work, the refuge will be maintained in its present state. There is reason to believe that the plant and animal life of the swamp have not been fully explored. On the other hand, it seems to be concluded that the ivory-billed woodpecker, for example, which once frequented its fastnesses, is now extinct, and at present there is some poaching. The "gators" are suffering most.

But let us turn from our misgivings over man's excesses in this remarkable region and consider the swamp itself. In Law

2

School, we once defined an unfamiliar legal concept in terms of what it was not. It may be well to think of the swamp in a like manner. The Okefinokee was *not* unhealthy. Its brownish, coffee-colored waters did not emanate noxious vapors and were, in fact, good to drink. After a few tentative sips Anne and I came to relish their slightly acid flavor. Our friends who lived on the edge of the swamp not only did *not* have malaria and sleeping-sickness, but were unusually healthy looking and singularly vigorous in action and speech. Cottonmouth moccasins did *not,* as a recent writer has inferred, lie in wait on every cypress knee for the unsuspecting voyageur. Anne and I have traveled more than one hundred thirty miles along the lakes and runs of the swamp and have yet to see a cottonmouth. One of our guides assured us that "a moccasin, when it is young is too small to harm you, and when it is old, is too lazy." He capped his disdain for them by habitually going barefooted. We saw but two snakes, both of which were harmless. There were some mosquitoes but they were much fewer than we expected and were not particularly annoying. And our guide, who thinks logically about the phenomena of swamp life, reasoned that the abundant fish of the swamp eat the mosquito larvae, thus keeping down their numbers.

The swamp was *not* completely dark, wholly gloomy, nor altogether forbidding. It had great variety. There were islands, lakes, the unique "prairies," streams and runs, as well as dense forests growing right out of the water. The islands which were fairly numerous but which did not occupy a very large portion of the total swamp area, were generally sandy and rose from a few inches to eight or ten feet above the water. One of the larger was Billy's Island, which embraced several hundred acres and supported a pine forest. The lakes were small but possessed

3

a startling limpidness. The sudden glimpse of the unruffled surface and exquisite reflections of one of these lakes, as one emerged unexpectedly from a run, was an unforgettable experience. It was surprising to us, who supposed that a swamp is stagnant, to find the water everywhere in motion, and often moving with surprising speed. Numerous times, as I was standing in front of the boat for a photograph, the particular scene which had caused me to stop would be swiftly and substantially altered by the drift.

Although they were hardly as extensive as the moss-draped forests of cypress, the "prairies" presented the unique landscapes of the swamp. They are called prairies, I suppose, because they look like prairies, being broad, open expanses, often square miles in extent, covered with low vegetation growing in the water. This vegetation was interspersed with water lilies, their leaves lying flat on the surface, with the pointed "never-wets" which if pushed under water always straightened up, but there were grasses and other plant life which in perspective gave the illusion of plains country.

It was in the prairies that we found the great-winged waterfowl whose presence there in considerable numbers prompted the creation of the Okefinokee Refuge. Stalking along the edges of the channels, or at rest in the trees, many of those birds were ungainly looking, but once in the air, without exception, their movement was a superlatively gracious spectacle. Their flight around the prairies in vast arcs, now in sight, now disappearing behind a clump of cypresses and now coming to rest in a flurry of wing beats, captivated us. Even though they moved swiftly, these great birds and the unhurried stroke of their wings seemed to epitomize with complete appropriateness the serene vitality of the swamp. We saw ibises,

4

egrets (now on the increase), great blue herons, little blue herons, ospreys, and others. We saw the untidy mass of the nest of a great blue heron in the top of a dead cypress. In a cypress bay, we saw the shadowy flight of one of the larger owls. Twice we heard the ear-splitting clatter of the pileated woodpecker, which the natives call the "lord god" bird. We saw the orange glint of a prothonotary warbler in flight. We missed the climax spectacle of all, a sandhill crane and his startling serenade.

We saw no bear or coon or deer, of which there are many, but did see several alligators. We found a small one near at hand and pushed into the swale for a photograph, only to see the alligator roll into the water and leave in a trail of bubbles. Each night our ear drums were tried by the din from innumerable frogs, more than twenty species of which have been recorded around the swamp.

I could dwell at length upon the dark gloom of the boat runs, twisting channels barely wide enough for the boat, winding oilily between the trunks of the cypresses and their protruding knees. Long skeins of Spanish moss brushed our faces and we swept innumerable spiderwebs from between the understory shrubs and trees. The brown, flaring trunks of the cypresses were everywhere, with their straight lines accented by the gray, perpendicularly hanging shreds of moss. There were few signs of man — one or two broken down, rotting trestles from the logging days; a gray, wooden tower used by surveyors, a rickety shelter along Minnie's Run built five feet above the ground by bygone fishermen. Beyond these, at the upper limits of Big Water, the swamp was still supreme, its scenery now ordered, now gathered into gray-green phantasies. Here was mystery we could not penetrate in a day or a week. Here was the climax forest, a paradox of land that merged into water and

5

of water that merged into land, an insoluble world of "trembling earth," of inexhaustible life, and of soul-stirring loveliness..

2

O UR INTRODUCTION to Isle Royale was by the *Disturbance of Grand Portage,* a two-engined cruiser under the captaincy of a young giant, Roy Oberg. I first saw him in long boots on top of a pile of ice, shunting ice into his boat. Disorder was everywhere — even in his hair, locks of which escaped from under an individualized hat drawn down across mischievous eyes. But there was no disorder in his navigating. He understood all the variables and had a reputation for making the eighteen mile trip from the mainland to the Isle regardless of fog and rain.

On the day we went over from Grand Portage on the western shore of Lake Superior just south of the Canadian boundary, it was rainy and cold. Air temperature by my pocket thermometer was 40° and the water temperature, 38°. Fog swirled up from the exhaust. Anne was bundled in an overcoat thoughtfully provided for her at Grand Portage. Oberg, now shaved and talkative, when I told him the water was 38° and not 32° as he predicted, said, "You've got a southern thermometer!"

The fog accumulated on the window in front of the wheel and the window was constantly cleared by a squeegee. Isle Royale lay, a low gray line, ahead.

Our first fishing trip on Lake Superior came the same afternoon. Our fishing friends trolled close to Isle Royale and with my field glasses I was able to get a close view of it. It had a rank, northern forest, remindful of the Smokies, but with an enormous amount of windfall. Fishing was poor. The catch on the two trips which we made was one lone lake trout. Even the commercial fishermen across the bay with their nets and lines were not catching many.

Although I tired of the fishing I loved the lake and the unbelievably frigid air. My hands became numb even though I had on four layers of jackets and sweaters. I was interested in the fog which rolled in and out. Three freighters appeared out of the mist, and there was a hoarse booming of the fog horn from the lighthouse. Two nights and a day we heard it at short intervals — ominous and excitint to me, a landsman.

In the always chill air I put in long hours splitting wood. It was scavenged along the lake, pulp wood which had gotten loose. It had been sawed into sixteen and twenty inch lengths.

There was a fine stand of fir on the island, and many paper birches which had to be fenced with chicken wire to foil the beavers. There were many stumps in that small, four acre island bearing the long-chiseled toothmarks of the beavers. We

8

watched the beavers several nights. A black head would appear on the surface of the inlet, followed by a slight wake in the water. Then something would scare it, and a simultaneous flap of the tail on the water and the *ker chung* of the dive would startle us. One night we heard a distinct mewing sound from a beaver well out in the inlet and we supposed it was warning a young one near the bank. It was eerie standing down on the dock in the chill air and partial moonlight watching for these black blobs to appear on the surface of the water. One night it was so cold I wore my host's huge, fleece-lined overcoat.

Occasionally we would hear a winter wren and a whitethroated sparrow. Of other birds we were not so sure, except for the "seagles" (sea gulls). We learned to pronounce the word like the natives. There were many of these birds. Their gray and white feathers were immaculate. Their flying fascinated me. I loved the way they made a short turn just at landing in order to face the wind. There were several fast boats on the lake, but I never saw one strike a bird. Occasionally the birds would move out of the way, but if there were even a few feet of clearance, they would float undisturbed. Their calls were high-pitched and querulous, but after a time I came to associate the calls with the whole lovely setting and I liked them. We saw the nest of a duck, a bare depression on the edge of the inlet, with two eggs, somewhat pointed but of the same volume as a hen's eggs with mottled green and brownish markings remindful of the jungle suits worn by the soldiers in the war.

Our richest experience was the view of two bald eagles on our trip to Washington Harbor on Isle Royale proper. Their majesty in this natural setting on the tip of a spruce near the shoreline of the inlet was something new and very exciting. We saw several loons, placidly floating on the mildly choppy water.

I have since read that they float on the roughest of water and lightly surmount the waves.

On our return trip to the mainland via the *Disturbance,* we were chilled to the bone. The air temperature was 40°. There was some fog and wind. The water calmed as we neared land, and its surface was broken by wave and quartering winds into myriad, shallow, spoonshaped pockets not much larger although somewhat longer than the hollow of a spoon. These ripples reflected the blue-green and rose of the sunset sky — each reflection, individual and perfect. Sometimes one side of this pocket caught the blue-green and the other side, the rose. These pockets were innumerable, creating a broken patchwork which but for the color reminded me of the fretwork on a loon's back. I wonder if the markings on the loons evolved as a protection in such waters in breeding season.

I came to love that island life — the fogs, the sense of being cut off. I came not to mind the noise of the boats. They were useful there. The inlets were the highways and the boats were the vehicles.

3

GRAND TETONS
SHEEP MOUNTAIN
WYOMING
1948

M Y FIRST hike into the Teton Mountains was to Death Canyon. The walls on either side of the entrance were vertical. In the back of my mind had been the thought of doing some rock climbing, and mentally I appraised each cliff with this in mind. Many of them looked impossible. Horrible, terrifying, vertical faces!

The size of the streams, and in their lower reaches, their fast-moving spirited rush, fascinated me. There had been no great amount of rain. There was no obvious water storage, although Bernie Frank assured me it was greater than I thought. And yet here were these turbulent, foaming, rushing streams. How could any amount of snow, much less those tiny patches hanging here and there on the slopes above supply such a mass of water. Later, we were to wade the stream in effecting a crossing and the volume of water did not then seem so great.

But my initial impressions of these streams were shot through with incredulity.

There were some mighty trees, bearing exotic names — Engelman spruce, lodgepole pine, Douglas fir. And there were those meadows, not always as smoothly grassy as they appeared, but nevertheless, gently lying, bright-green, and in repose, accented by this strangely sparse pattern of evergreens — a delight to the eye and soul which fulfilled every expectation.

Despairing of reaching the divide, we turned from the stream to a rocky outcrop and meadow toward the head of the canyon. There the slopes were less precipitous, had a thin coating of soil, and bore a few herbaceous plants. Even so, the ascent was steep and I labored painfully and breathlessly upward. Again with higher climbs in mind, I wondered where I should find the strength or will.

On the trip to Lake Solitude two days later, we saw several rabbit-eared conies scampering about. On one huge rock bar through which the trail went, we saw three or four marmots. One of the marmots was sitting erect on its hind quarters. Its somber brown fur with a few black markings and flowing silhouette made one think of a monk in his robes.

Higher up, the stream was lazier than the one which boomed out of Death Canyon, but we saw so much snow some of my incredulity as to the source of these streams was dissipated.

Lake Solitude was still largely frozen over but had a few breaks in its ice, which revealed awesomely dark and deep water below — water with a limpid clarity which supplied exquisite reflections of the surrounding peaks.

A major impression of this hike was that of getting back

12

deep into the Tetons. We walked up toward, passed, and got miles back of the Grand Teton and of Mt. Owen and Teewinot and looked at them from the back side. Wondrous, beautiful, frightening pyramids which filled me with exaltation.

It was not my lot to climb to the top of any of the Teton peaks, but my next excursion high onto the Teton Glacier in the company of Bernie Frank, supplied sensational experiences. This glacier is in a high pocket surrounded by lofty pyramids. Early in the day it was already in deep shadows cast by the massive bulk of "The Grand" itself. No wonder a glacier formed up there.

The very thought of ice axes frightened me, and Olaus Murie's solemn warning that snow slopes could be very dangerous was obviously based on personal experience. We rented a couple of axes from Glen Exum, chief guide in the Park, and took a leisurely pace up the switchbacks. I was never winded or in distress the entire day.

Bernie and I tried out our axes on a short snow slope just over the divide from Amphitheatre Lake. I learned my lesson quickly. The snow was steeper than I had thought. I started to slide uncontrollably and in terror I dug in the point of my ax and came to a heartening, if inglorious, stop.

As we moved out onto the steeper slopes, we very carefully punched holes with our heels, bracing ourselves with our axes. Gradually we gained confidence, but if we erred it was on the side of caution and not of heedlessness.

Across the slope of the first moraine, we diligently cut steps with our axes, but edged as soon as practicable over to the rocks, upon which we each felt more at home. With my hobbed shoes, which I had also gotten from Exum, I had all the

14

confidence of a cat on those roughly fractured and unweathered stones and boulders. How long ago had they been dropped by the glacier? And how many eons had the smoothly worn stones in the beds of our Smoky Mountain streams been polishing? One gets a new measure of nature's processes in such a place.

I was struck by the jade-green, opaque, and lustreless surface of Delta Lake as it lay far below the glacier catching its milky silt in the outflow.

On the glacier itself we did away with packs and ice axes as we moved freely over its broad, smooth, and almost level floor. We had been told that there were no crevasses. Soon after I left my pack and started after Bernie, I was caught in a violent surge of wind which momentarily throttled my breath. What a pygmy I seemed in such raw, violent surroundings. But the wind did not persist and I walked easily far up onto the glacier. It was covered with a sort of granular snow, or sleet, which had melted away from around a great boulder and, as we jumped into the pit for a drink of water, I observed that the side walls were dirty-gray ice. Face to face with a glacier! Quite an experience for a Smoky Mountaineer!

North, west, and south the views from that glacial pocket were straight up. I wondered if I would ever do any real rock climbing! To the east the views took in the width of Jackson Hole. We could see Timber Island, the dark streak along the Snake River, the upper end of the Black Tail Butte, and the wide sweep of the sagebrush to the mountains on the far side — Sheep Mountain and the Gros Ventre slide.

On the way down I shouted a bear away at Amphitheatre. The bear was in dead earnest — he was running toward me on the gallop chasing a small animal. But my ice ax, which I instinctively raised, must have looked dangerous and my voice,

15

which I also instinctively raised, must have sounded discordant. The bear desisted, much to my relief, and disappeared between two boulders. It did not leave, because as we passed down the trail we saw it again, nosing around the campsites, scavenging.

Coming down the switchbacks in the early twilight we saw the shadows of the Tetons creeping in a jagged front across the still sunlit plains of Jackson Hole. We could identify them. That massive shadow in the lead was from "The Grand" itself.

SHEEP MOUNTAIN

Later, with Olaus and Mardy Murie, Anne and I visited an area of mesas and canyons, which has been as little touched by man as any place I know. It was Sheep Mountain on the eastern rim of Jackson Hole. We started out in a little ravine where there was a spring and some trees. Back of us were huge stretches of sagebrush. Plodding upward by hollow and ridge top, we passed through upland meadows which had fairly exploded into bloom. As individuals, the flowers were delicate, but they grew in such masses that they threw a wash of color over the whole mountain — yellows and blues and reds. There were wild phlox and gilia and paintbrush and sun flowers and numerous others.

Across the shimmering plain of Jackson Hole, the Tetons did not look so much like scissor-sharp cut-outs in gray and white, as they often do, but were pale blue and intriguing under the white of their many-faced peaks. Once we stumbled up a rock bar and into an evergreen woods, full of blowdowns. Once we were held up by a delicately blooming orchis.

Olaus was a joy to be with. He knew every plant, every bird,

16

every animal. With all the knowledge of the Indian and perhaps much of his feeling, Olaus looked at this environment with intelligence and understanding.

The air, rushing in, found the depths of our lungs as we moved above 10,000, above 11,000, feet. The Tetons were now a faded sierra on the west. We paused on a bench, by a snowdrift. Below us was a rounded, dry-looking canyon. Three hundred feet above us, the top was a mass of loose rocks and boulders. We left our packs, puffed up over the rocks, keeping away from the unstable edge at the head of the canyon. Under the stones and rubble, there was a stratification of limestone, which we were to learn was weathered by the wind into needles and blades which would tear our hands at a touch.

Beyond us was an unsuspected country — as different as light and dark from what we had left — a country of broad mesas, eaten into by canyons — a hard, sharp, dry, and fascinating country, nondescript in color and planless in pattern. This was the country we had been brought to see — the summer range of the wild sheep. Each mesa edge had a flowing skirt of talus a thousand feet deep. Trees crept up into the canyons. But on top the vegetation seemed so seared by the heat that it crackled in the wind. How could sheep thrive on such fare — and where was the succulence which would keep the fluids alive in their bodies?

We had to leave the top — it was getting late. We planned to traverse the length of Sheep Mountain and camp in the upper end of one of the canyons. The wind tore at us and the chill penetrated as we clambered down that rock pile to our packs. There was no man-made trail, but Olaus, for sure footing, was looking for a wild sheep trail to take us under those sheer cliffs of crumbling limestone. The broad bosom we had ascended dwindled and he led us onto a narrowing, steeply tilted bench under a wild jumble of rocks which had broken off the upper strata. The way led into this jumble and its evil slope dropped terrifyingly and disappeared beneath us.

Olaus was baffled. His memory had played a trick upon him. No sheep trail was discernible through that awful jumble, and at length he led us up this shifting slope of barren rocks. They were rough and sharp, and our boots held well, but they were in frightening repose. Once the rock upon which I stepped shifted with me. Another was moving a few yards to my right and a movement caught my eye to the left. Mardy was below me, a tiny figure among these baleful stones, any one of which could have crushed her. Would this terrible mass crunch into motion and pour over the steeps below, carrying us along with it, as scrambling and terrified we made a mad effort to keep from being caught and ground into a pulp?

That I am writing this is evidence that we were spared that eventuality. Actually, we worked our way almost in sight of the top again — not from the stable west, but from the unsettled south. Olaus found a gap in the cliff edge; we scrambled down onto fine scree beside loose boulders which could have crushed us and eventually found ourselves on a rib of mother rock. Around a corner under the cliffs, and hanging above other appalling slopes, we found the sheep trail. It was hardly discernible, about as wide as my hand, but it was firm!

A few nights before, in an amazing movie of wild sheep in action taken by Adolph Murie, we had seen sequences of sheep running along such slopes and the camera was so close we could see their hoofs feeling for a safe footing, just as a person would try a loose board before setting foot upon it. How many times had this thin trace we were on been tried by sheep to provide this narrow band of continuous security? Even so it was not easy walking under overnight packs. We would stagger, and reach out to the cliffs to steady ourselves and rip our hands on knife-edged surfaces. It was getting late and the cliffs stretched far ahead of us. Once I glanced back. The Tetons stood out against the fiery glare of the setting sun. I called to the others and their nerves were as edged as those sand-honed rocks:

"What does he want?" they said sharply.

And as I looked ahead at the pitch of the slope, I wondered if I could do it — but it was never as bad as it looked. Those blessed sheep had always found firm footing.

I wondered how long our day could last. It was getting dark and we were still not out of it. Eventually we turned a corner and found ourselves on a broader, arching slope which led to the mesas. But we needed water, and in the darkness we plunged down through a shadowy world of rolling stones, cliff surfaces, vegetation, and trees — to a grassy bench where there were dead trees for a fire and a rivulet for water. It was 9:30. We had been at it for twelve hours. We built a warming fire and had supper in its belching shadows. We had lost much time; we were so weary we simply sat and stared. We crept gratefully into our sleeping bags, and under stars which did not twinkle we found our rest. The next morning our tarps were gray with frost.

4

I N THE Olympic National Park the field trip took us to the rain forest on the Pacific side of the Park. We went first up the lower stretches of the Hoh River and then four of us — Preston Macy, Superintendent of the Park, Howard Zahniser, Richard Leonard, and I walked five miles through a cut-over section of the lower Bogachiel valley to the Bogachiel Ranger Station, where we camped.

I loved some of the Olympic names — Queets, Quinnalt, Hoh, Elwha, and Bogachiel. Zahnie commented that the name, Bogachiel, was worth a thousand names like Smith, when it came to enlisting conservation interest. The names were savory with the magnetism of this new country. By contrast, Mt. Olympus seemed flat and banal as a name, and fraught with associations which seemed alien to that unique country. In some ways, it did not seem unique country either. It was my

first view of one of the great rain forests. Those great slim trees were a delight to the eye. But the mossiness and the giant ferns were remindful of the Okefinokee, and of pocket-sized versions of the same thing in the Smokies. The Olympics did not seem awesomely forbidding to me as did the Tetons.

The trees belied their great size because of their glorious proportions. I hardly should have guessed that some were two hundred sixty-five feet high had not Dick Leonard and John Spencer paced one which had fallen, upending a root system fifty feet long and thirty feet high. The roots seemed to go proportionately deeper into the ground than those found in the Smokies, where so many of the evergreens are found growing almost on bare rock. But the fallen giants, giving life to thousands of seedlings, were similar to those in the Smokies, except that in the Smokies there would be greater variety of species taking root on the down trees. Aerial roots were common. Many trees had rooted on a dead trunk sending down their roots to the ground. Then the trunk rotted away leaving the young trees standing on stilts.

But those great aisles and avenues between the gigantic boles of straight and silent firs and spruces were utterly unique and reminded me of nothing I had seen before. The trunks were shapely, tapering gradually to fluffy crowns. The enormous cedars, with flat systems of needles like the white cedar of the north country, contributed an exotic, almost tropical tone to the woods. It seemed to me that the trees in the Bogachiel were more uniform, and smaller than those up the Hoh. There was more ruggedness and more ancientness up the Hoh. But the feeling we had in the Bogachiel valley, in moving mile after mile through a perfectly flat valley with those straight forms standing in irregular ranks and making cavernous enclosures of space in every direction, was unmatched. I am glad that we could travel on foot — measuring our puny strength against its vastness.

There was a richness about it. On the day previously we had hiked five miles to the ranger station. Part of the distance had been through logged-over areas — places of grayness, dead limbs, dead boles, washings, and of torn, lifeless soil. There was a deadness about it — an air of utter neglect, a spectacle of heedlessness. The waste was appalling. Gray log butts eight feet in diameter, twenty-four feet long, cracked in the sun. They had been left to disintegrate presumably because they had an unsightly or inconvenient knot. This waste of wood was spiritually devastating. Men had sought to convert the green life and repose of the forest we were in, to the dead grayness of the forest we had left, because of the "shortage" of lumber. Why had they not used up what they had abandoned? Some of the stumps were twelve and fifteen feet above the ground. Why was all that wood unused? Was it because the graceful flare and taper of the trunk which gave it such an air of belonging to the ground could not go through the mills? Why was there no way of saving that too? We were told that the firs would not seed in their own shade — that the forest had to be leveled to start the great cycle of growth which would produce another forest many years hence. But what of the human generations between the peaks of the forest cycle? Will they be deprived of an experience with this divine forest?

5

FLAT TOPS
DINOSAUR NATIONAL MONUMENT
MAROON BELLS
COLORADO
1950

ANNE AND I first reached timber line at Loveland Pass, between Denver and Glenwood Springs, Colorado. There were patches of snow lying here and there on the tenuous green herbaceous carpet. We climbed from the saddle to try our lungs, and saw the most delicate and exquisite of alpine flowers growing at the very surface of the earth, flat against it. There was a deep, lively blue forget-me-not, a rich magenta-colored creeping phlox, and a bloom of delicate white. There was lupine also, but those shy, exquisite low-growing things attracted me as nothing I had ever seen. At the pass I again saw old friends, the marmots, and played hide and seek with one which had a hole at the foot of a snowdrift. It would slide to safety from its perch on the drift each time it saw me.

My experience with timber line in the Flat Tops Primitive Area in north central Colorado a week later is hazy in my memory — largely I think because I viewed it from the back of a horse. I had my doubts about using a horse. But I wanted the experience, since I find myself so often in conflict with those who want more horse trails in the Smokies, and because of the recent utterances of a back-sliding hiker that the only way to see mountain country is from horseback.

But I was not convinced. I freely admit that I was not as tired as I would otherwise have been when we lunched at ten thousand feet after a ten mile ride up from the seventy-five hundred foot level. I might even admit that it is a good way to "see" country. But I felt that it was not a good way to "feel" country. I am sure that Ernest Griffith, who walked the full twenty-three miles and who slogged through the boggy tundra on top, must carry back intimate impressions which can not be mine. And as I look back on it, I seem somehow detached from my memories of that incomparable, rolling mountaintop country.

Although there were bold headlands that rose above this rolling tundra, somehow the impression I carried back was that this country was not too rugged and though uninhabited at the time, not too remote. I am sure that the wilderness feeling — the remoteness — the impression of extremes — would have rested with me if, breathless and slightly taxed, I had moved across that exotic plain under my own power. For I know in my mind it was not mild country, but wild country, just emerging from winter, where the new growth on the shrubs along the rim was just beginning to show, and where a few weeks before there had been little but a blanket of snow and outcropping ledges and rocks.

I wish now I had walked — if not all the way — then, part of the way — at my own speed, soaking up the odors and intimate sights and sounds of that great country.

DINOSAUR NATIONAL MONUMENT

In retrospect, it is difficult to say just what I expected to see when I visited Dinosaur National Monument. I know that I expected rough, hot country. I expected canyons. But my thought was disembodied — there was no real connection between me and what I was to see. It was like the impression one gets of terrain from an airplane. The country is like a map — stylized — with only the great features and all the roughnesses and imperfections eliminated.

We met our host, Dave Canfield, Superintendent of Rocky Mountain National Park and of Dinosaur National Monument, at Jensen, Utah and were immediately taken to monument headquarters about six miles away, across the Colorado state line.

As we set off through that dry, seared country toward the headquarters, I knew I was in for something new in the way of experiences. Even the drive through the deserts of southeastern Utah two years before was not like this. There was something inescapable, almost malevolent, in this searing, blasting heat and brightness.

We met Jess Lombard, the ranger in charge of the monument, and walked the scorching two hundred yards to the quarry where the stratification had yielded up so many dinosaur remains. There were no trees. There was a sandy path with bleak mountains all around, and a number of bright-blooming flowers. The dinosaur-yielding strata faced us like a wall. Several

26

perfect skeletons had been removed. Exposed remains were only fragmentary – a knee-joint, a vertebra.

Our first view of the Green River was late in the afternoon, where the stream emerged from the canyon. Here we found shade. There were riffles in the water, and the air which had seemed to be drawing the very moisture from my body was here friendly and temperate, and my body seemed to recapture it from the air.

That night it rained. Superintendent Canfield expressed some hesitance about taking those old roads up to Blue Mountain from which we could visit Round Top and have views down into the canyons from above. But though the sky was overcast, there was no more rain.

We went through sagebrush country which I had seen before and for which, on this trip, I was to gain a wholesome respect bordering upon affection. Blue Mountain was plateau-like, a rolling blue-green sea of sagebrush. On the ascent we went through sparse forests of juniper and of pinyon pine and attained a rough elevation of 7700 feet.

The sky was still heavy with clouds and when we emerged upon rocky, treeless Round Top the gorge was filled with mist. I was not expecting fog or mist in desert country.

But the fog rolled away, very dramatically. We looked down into a maze of rugged country, and at great thick strata emerging from under Blue Mountain at a slight tilt and rising gradually to an abrupt edge which marked the canyons. But the scene was so tortured, that in looking across the country and not directly down at it, it was long before we made sense of what lay before us. Finally Dick and I picked out a promontory at an equal elevation – Harper's Corner. From the map we could tell that it overlooked the Green just below the forks with the Yampa. Then we discovered Steamboat Rock far beneath Harper's Corner, and these landmarks furnished the key to what we saw. But I did not then discern the tiny side canyons which split the great bordering plateau, down which we went later in the day to river level at Echo Park.

There was rich color in what we saw, a blueness in the distance, rivaling the blue of eastern mountains, but with more purple in it. Closer at hand there were wilder, more violent colors — reds, yellows, and light, sandy browns.

In the afternoon in two small trucks we plunged off the side of Blue Mountain to the tilted plateau. It had not rained there. Dust was inches deep on the road and swirled about us. Down one of those hidden canyons we entered a weird, exciting world of rock — great battlements, gendarmes, alcoves and hard, clean, tempting slopes. One could spend days there, just climbing and trying to climb.

We stopped at a little oasis deep in the rock and walked through cottonwoods to the canyon wall. High above us on an unweathered vertical surface were pictographs of pleasing outline pecked into the stone. How old were they? How had the artists mounted to that height and supported themselves for the lengthy task? Were they old men or young men who did it? What was stirring their minds? Were they crude ventures at art — or were they stories in stone?

Dave stopped again. He seldom said anything. It was up to us to see what was to be seen. We were almost at the mouth of the descending side canyon. Below us in the center of the vista was a great monolith — Steamboat Rock. It overhung the junction of the Green and Yampa rivers and was responsible for one of the major twists of the Green below the forks.

As we entered the main canyon, we felt again the welcome moisture from the river. The outer bend was compassed by a massive wall of rock a thousand feet high. Between it and the river was a level park-like plain with grass and scattered trees. Across the river in the inner bend was this long wall of rock, to which the river clung on three sides, Steamboat Rock. The great rounded bend was Echo Park, or Pat's Hole. We could see the junction of the two rivers, each emerging from its own private, fantastic canyon. The rivers were placid here. It was the rock twisted like taffy which seemed violent and tumultuous. Only the great perpendicular walls of the bend, dwarfing us like pygmies on the river plain, seemed in repose and above violence.

I puffed up the slopes between plain and wall and was aware of the near mile elevation. Below me was the pleasant park-like plain. At my back was that incredible wall, and broadside across from me was Steamboat Rock.

The scene was so tremendous, I was glad at first I did not know too much about the geology. I wanted to absorb it as a thing of beauty without the leavening of sophistication and knowledge. The proposed dam would be a couple of miles down river on the other side of Steamboat Rock and the water would fill the vast cirque and mount half way up those vertical cliffs. What a taming of that vast scene!

Around the other side of the bend, Dick and I followed a cattle trail along a ledge at the foot of the cliffs which fell from the side of Harper's Corner, and went down-river until we could see the beginning of its bend around Harper's Corner. We looked longingly across at Steamboat Rock and discussed ways of climbing it. Climber that he was, Dick paid his sincere respects to those who had scrambled along the crest and had raised the cairn at its head. At our farthest advance down the river, we tried out the echoes of this great basin. Our shouts carried easily between the rocky walls to the others in our party who were barely visible to us.

The sky was overcast as we drove out of the canyon, but the road was still deep with dust. Again there was that distant aspect, a bewitching green-blue, where the sun lit up the valleys under the clouds. Four members of The Wilderness Society Council — Olaus Murie, Ernest Griffith, Dick Leonard, and I — were seated together in the back of one of the pick-up trucks. We were excited by the superb scenery and magnificent setting of Echo Park and discussed the threat to the canyon. The dust swirled about us, got into our clothes and caked on our faces and arms. Dick Leonard summed it up:

"It's worth saving; we've got to fight for it."

And his remark, coming out of the moving cloud of dust which engulfed our truck, was the very first action in the years' long campaign to save Dinosaur.

The second morning, in trucks, we pushed out an ever diminishing way through the sagebrush along one of the fingers of Blue Mountain. After miles of this the way became impossible, and we hiked through pines and sagebrush toward Harper's Corner. The soil was gravelly and became more rocky as we proceeded. To our right was the vast gulf around Steamboat Rock, where we had been the previous afternoon. It had an appealing blueness through the trees. Overhead the sun blazed through magnificently piled clouds.

The ridge became more narrow, the trees sparser and the ground beneath our feet became solid rock, which dropped away frighteningly on either side.

The point itself was crumbling at the edges into mere

30

chunks of rock which rested loosely upon each other. A disintegrating neck of these loose boulders had almost severed the actual point or corner from the main body of the ridge and I temporarily lost my sense of balance as I came to this place, although others, including Anne, crossed it easily.

The sun burned down on the treeless point and the stupendous view met our eyes in unrelieved nakedness. To the west there was comparative order in the deep, straight gash of the Green River canyon. But to the north and east, the valleys were twisted and tortured beyond belief. Great solid layers of mesa broke into plunging canyons and the intervening mountains were so drawn by stresses that I was again impressed that they looked like ropes and hunks of brown and yellow taffy. It was a Vulcan's pit of creation — raw, baking, and shouting out its story of time and violence.

There was little conversation. Those scenes spoke to us louder than our own futile thoughts. The vastness made pygmies of us, and its savage beauty uprooted our sense of values. I wondered if the person who had proposed a dam had ever stood tiny and alone upon this point!

As we broke camp about mid-afternoon, getting the cars to moving through the deeply rutted sand, the clouds which had been hugging Blue Mountain closely and darkly through the morning broke into rain and that thin, loose soil formed a skim of the slickest and at the same time the gummiest mud I have ever encountered. We had hardly topped the first "swell" in this ocean of sagebrush when we spotted the two trucks wallowing in a trough ahead of us. No road was visible around them. They seemed half submerged in the brush. Four of us went out on foot to the rescue, slipping and sliding in the mud of the roadway. Where we could, we walked in the rain-drenched brush. One truck was still mobile and it was maneuvered to a firmer place in the brush. Chains were attached and a rope broken out. Ultimately by man and motor power, the second truck slithered to firm ground.

We slogged back to the other cars and decided to take another fork. The cars quickly broke through the muddy surface. Mud and dust combined to balloon great layers of soil around our tires until they bulged like colossal doughnuts. We reached an impasse. Two more cars bogged down. We laid a couch of brush alongside the rear wheels to assist us in applying chains. The brush was drenched with moisture, but broke easily in usable quantities and we got the chains on. Lombard pushed ahead in his truck using it as a mud breaker. The other two cars followed, gaining momentum where they could in that streaming mud. And when they burst from the ruts, the cars would careen from the road into the brush and back again. At times, they would leap the road as they lurched back and would take off into the brush on the opposite side. Never have I seen such uncontrollable driving. It was exciting and neck-popping but safe, since there was no traffic, and banks and gullies along the road were nonexistent. The cars seemed as much at ease in the brush as on the road. At each high point we waited for the others to catch up.

We finally intercepted the trucks. Combining our eight man power, we managed to make better progress. Lombard was in the lead — mud-breaking and burning the cab with slightly damp, desert profanity. Up one grade, his chains could not dig through the mud far enough for traction. Three of us rode the rear bumper to give the truck added weight — and we would plow forward fifteen feet, back up, and get a running start to make fifteen feet more.

There were times when it tooked as though we might have to spend the night in the cars awaiting the drying of the mud. Dick Leonard's eyes shone. He loved the primitive, impersonal combat with the mud and so did I. At the last serious grade, Olaus's tires had become so heavily plastered with mud that each was over a foot across. I pried great hunks of mud four inches thick from them. As Olaus wallowed along in Lombard's tracks, his motion finally ceased. We tried to push him out of the ruts into the brush but the car was too heavy and unwieldy. We pulled great piles of brush and laid them into the ruts. Skidding alongside we got him to better ground at the top of the grade. Dave Canfield pouring on the gas, lurched forward like some great, erratic bullet and also won the summit.

The whole incident had its comical aspects — our being bogged down in mud in the middle of a desert! It was a gleeful anomaly to me. How could mud at the same time be so utterly yielding and so utterly clinging!

MAROON BELLS PRIMITIVE AREA

Leaving that desert country and our lusty companions, Anne and I went off to further adventures in the mountains of north central Colorado. Bernie Frank and Joe Penfold had told us of the Maroon Bells-Snowmass Primitive Area. We thought we might camp at Maroon Lake and hike up to Crater Lake and perhaps to Buckskin Pass. But when we arrived at Maroon Lake early in the afternoon and saw the scores of cars, we did not even weigh the point. We hastily packed, and at nine thousand feet set out for what we hoped would be the solitude of Crater Lake a thousand feet higher. Where is there any great wilderness left? Cars and roads and horses rub elbows with every wilderness I have seen out west. There is more honest remoteness in the jungled forests of the Smokies.

We made good time on the up-trail – perhaps better time than was sensible at that elevation and under those packs, for I was very tired the next day. Perhaps we were excited – pushing out without companions into those great mountains. Perhaps we were a bit proud of our ability to carry our loads and camp where we pleased without benefit of horses. We met one horseback party and three small hiking parties – but saw no evidence of overnight packs. The forest about us was not too handsome and the valley above us was barricaded by a great gaunt rock bar, upon which were some straggly trees, and which impounded Crater Lake.

As we mounted this, we glimpsed the lake. There were sand and rock bars and low marshes at its lower end. We proceeded along an easy path through the woods on the west side to its upper end. We crossed and waded several streams which were fed by the innumerable snow fields above us. These streams were clear and lively and very cold. The spruce patches were attractive at a distance, but the forest floor had been trampled down by over-camping and we went on to a copse of small spruces at the upper end. Here we searched at length for a place to pitch our tent and found none. The scant ground cover was underlain with jagged rock. Evidently the forest and vegetation were just beginning to cover the center of the great U-shaped slopes of scree which had tumbled from the ledges high above us. There was no view of the lake from the copse and we retraced our steps to a small meadow along the west side near a stream and near the upper end.

It was a happy choice. There was a view of the lake, which

was only twenty feet away, and the stream was hardly farther. A fallen spruce at the same distance supplied an abundance of wood and above us, in plain view, were the deeply furrowed pyramids of the Maroon Bells. We saw only one human visitor in two days and three nights; we saw a deer and a bear across the lake, and had a nightly visit by a beaver on our side of the lake.

We had hardly pitched our tent and eaten, when we climbed a little knoll back of the tent and spotted the deer browsing on a steep slope across from us. Back at camp, I saw a wake in the water and the high ripple in front of a fast-swimming beaver. We scared him away through our very eagerness to glimpse him at close hand. And then as deep dusk settled, Anne said,

"I see something moving in the brush across the lake."

With the binoculars, we could see a large black bear. He disappeared in a patch of woods and although we had no real fear, we knew he could cause an "incident" if he smelled our bacon. We decided to close it tightly in a can, bury the can in the depths of the large knapsack and leave the knapsack on a rock near the tent. Five minutes later, we were relieved to pick up the bear, again through the glasses — scrambling over the rocks and scree at the upper end of the lake, and moving directly up the main canyon away from us.

The valley we were in at Crater Lake was narrow with mountains literally all around us — across the lake, up and down the main canyon, and sheerly above us on our side.

The Maroon Bells were laminated in broad thick layers terminating in impossible ledges. Over the ages chunks of rock had broken off the ledges and rolled down to the valley, coming to rest in wide sweeping rock beds. Up canyon the cross section was distinctly U-shaped, with the high cliffs forming the side of

35

the U and the rock bars, the wide curve. Snow lay high on every ledge and water poured off in waterfalls, both east and west of us.

These high slopes were deceptive. They looked easily climbable, and looked as though they might shelter high little lakes back of their edges. But through the binoculars some of these slopes jumped into cavernous, forbidding amphitheatres of disintegrating rock.

On the first morning I went up-canyon into the rocks. The rocks were of all colors and sizes — greens and reds, and chunks as big as a small room. There was no real stability — the smaller ones often gave under my weight. I had a vague thought of crossing the stream and of walking completely around the lake, but the stream was much larger than it had appeared from our camp and was uncrossable without a drenching. No wonder the bear, on the evening before, had been so single-minded in going up-canyon instead of across the canyon.

The lake water was clear but in all the time we were there, I saw no sign of fish. The bottom seemed grassy at the upper end but there was a barren quality to it. A man told us later, "You'll never find fish in such a lake."

Monday we loafed except for my picture taking and Anne's descent to the car for a few more supplies. That night the beaver showed up early and as he came to our side of the lake we observed him from behind a screen of aspens.

We went to bed before the sun had left the peaks. In that high country, we rose early and went to bed early. That night it rained and the water ran under our tent.

Up early, we decided to climb to Buckskin Pass. All the way up the clouds were magnificent, hiding the crags of the Maroon Bells.

The tundra area above timber line fascinated me. There was such a cleanness about it. The vegetation grew to the very edges of the fretwork of streams which gathered from the main snow fields and everything was open and visible. It could hardly be called bleak at this time of year with the tiny flowers in bloom. But the thinness of the air, the ragged cliffs and snow fields, plus the meagerness of the vegetation, made for a wild, exotic quality. I climbed very slowly, not forcing myself; Anne, even more slowly.

The trail had many switchbacks which shortened as we got higher, finally lost itself under a high snow bank. We worked around this and came out onto the pass, wide and rounded, half covered with clinging, low, scant vegetation and half with snow. Snowmass to the west was unmistakable – a rough, rugged mountain with an immense snow field above the dim, greenish surface of Snowmass Lake. Black clouds boiled ominously above all these peaks west of us and they were hanging lower on the Maroon Bells, now quite near and to the south of us. Below us in the valley was the familiar braided pattern of fast-rushing, snow-fed streams. I climbed the south col as the clouds covered Snowmass and swept toward us.

Back at the pass we ate hurriedly and crept down behind a bank of earth with our feet on the snow bank out of a biting wind. The wind grew in force and presently pellets of sleet bounced on the snow. Fog blotted the mountains before us, and becoming chilled we decided to descend. As we stood up the full fury of the wind hit us and the sleet bit into our skin like splinters of glass. This was an above-timberline world and the pleasant meadow-like aspect of the gap in the warm sunshine with the brilliant creeping flowers had been misleading. My head and ears were protected by a nor'wester. I had on a wool shirt and jacket and was otherwise protected by a flapping poncho, but the cold and thinness of the air and the raging wind sapped our body warmth and as we scrambled around the end of the snow field to begin the descent, we were thoroughly chilled.

Below the pass on the steep downward switchbacks, we saw again the body of a horse which we had passed on the way up. It had died almost at the pass. A shallow niche had been scooped out for it. A bit of soil had been shoveled over it, but its legs and hoofs stuck out grotesquely. I thought how forlorn is death in a place like that – a place too austere and rough even for burial.

But I think I can understand why Olaus Murie has said,

"I like timber line the best of all."

There is a spaciousness and aloneness about it – just raw, primal matter, and the elements. The oft-time evil complexities of civilization are nonexistent, and likewise, its warmth and security. Here one was on his own, without shelter and support and something in the soul rose to the challenge.

Down at the lake, we found our bacon gone. Anne suspected the bear, but I found no traces. There were tiny, muddy footprints along the side of the tent. I suspected a marmot.

We had an early supper and kept a lookout for the beaver. It came early. It approached the lakeshore not one hundred feet from our camp, and unsuspecting, came almost entirely out of the water and rested on the base of its tail and hind legs. It held a small length of aspen in its front paws and ate the bark, much as a human would eat corn off a cob. Its fur was stringy where the water ran off him, and in color it was a muddy, gray brown. After it left I examined the place and found many small branches of aspen eaten clean of bark, lying in the edge of the water, and as my eyes were further opened saw the trails through the weeds where it had dragged down limbs and trunks from the knoll back of our camp.

The beaver swam also in the early morning, although whether it ate then also, we can not testify. It never popped its tail on the water as did those at Isle Royale, but there were more people at Isle Royale, and more beavers. This one for all we observed was alone. We were amused as it swam toward one of the snags which had washed down into the lake in a freshet. It did not swim around it, but simply dived and came up on the other side.

I picked up a small length of aspen upon the bark of which the beaver had been eating. Examination disclosed an interesting thing. There were five cuts on it. Every cut but one, which was small and only a quarter of an inch across, was made at an angle of approximately 45° to the cross-section. Cutting at an angle entailed considerably more slicing but the beaver knew what every woodsman knows, that wood cuts more easily if cut at an angle.

That night I was again in my sleeping bag before dark. Sometime in the night I was awakened and became aware that the tent had collapsed. The rawhide thong which held up the tent pole had broken (could it have been eaten?) and the pole had fallen between us. Neither of us was touched. The pole was not heavy, but could have given us a nasty crack, had it fallen across our heads. I lay there for a moment looking up at the stars, and was surprised at how much of the world they occupied. In daylight the valley had seemed narrow between towering mountains. That night the mountains seemed to flatten out under this world of stars. From the warmth of my

39

sleeping bag, I laid the pole over the side of the tent, and the rest of the night we lay with our heads out-of-doors, whence between naps and turnings on the hard ground we looked out into infinite space.

At daybreak the beaver made another crossing of the lake. As we cooked breakfast, we dried the condensed moisture from our sleeping bags and tent, and by eight a.m. were packed and ready for the trip back to the world of men. At the lower end of the lake a fat, calm old marmot stood on its hind legs and watched us walk by, not ten feet away — a self-appointed doorkeeper to this wilder-land of lake and mountains and pass.

6

GREAT SMOKY MOUNTAINS
NORTH CAROLINA · TENNESSEE
1951

THURSDAY was bright and warm. We had incredible luck on the weather, and the trip was timed to the very peak of the fall season of color. At New Found Gap the ridges shimmered away, blue and glowing, to unreachable horizons. We picked up our packs and were off to the wilds, four of us in our forties — Olaus in his sixties. We headed east on Benton MacKaye's Appalachian Trail.

The woods were extraordinary. The centers of the valleys were like a brilliant tapestry and distant cut-over slopes glowed with color. The sun was warm at Charlies Bunion where we ate and clambered over the rocks. Beyond it we moved along a narrow ridge crest above steeply dropping valleys.

The Greenbrier valleys in particular were stunningly variegated in their lower reaches. Fingers of color — the hardwood — reached up the centers along the creeks, a colorful intrusion in the deep, somber greens of the conifers. Burned-over ridges on the Carolina side were a uniform purple in the late afternoon sun, where whole mountainsides had grown up with the same limited variety of saplings.

George Marshall remarked at the Bunion that the Greenbrier did not live for him until he looked down into it, vast and remote, from above. Olaus and Dick Leonard said early in the hike that they had not visualized walking through forested country along the divide. They had been conditioned to the high mountain meadows and timber-line country of the west.

At Charlies Bunion as we stood looking out over the forest, Dick remarked that it was the most extensive primeval forest he had ever seen. I did not question him at the time but wondered later if the forest we were looking at was greater than some of the vast reaches which had greeted us from the Soleduck Pass in the Olympics.

Olaus was very quiet, admitting later to chills and fever. He hiked somewhat more slowly than the rest and was not his usual, genial, appreciative self. At Laurel Top since it was getting late, Dick Leonard and I sped ahead to try to get to the shelter and to get a fire started by dark.

Wood there was — a fallen beech near the shelter. We got a fire started. He yodeled several times and finally we heard the others as they came over the rim of the ridge. Zahnie said our shouts came from so far down the slope they wondered at first if they had missed the trail.

Olaus went to bed after a cup of soup and remarked afterwards, he thought he was in paradise when thus at last he was able to relax.

The next morning there was fine color in the sunrise which was strained through the finely branching birches and beeches

42

below the shelter. Olaus was much more cheerful. All of us had slept well.

We spent an hour on Eagle Rocks and then pushed on in a leisurely manner. There was some discussion about the areas of dead forest. Dick spoke of them as "burns." This I challenged, saying I had never known of a fire in that vicinity. He asked what caused them. I said, maturity. This he challenged, I think rightly, since they were really too small for maturity in an area where the spruces could and did reach a remarkable size. We decided it must have been due to sporadic insect infestation or windfall.

Olaus pointed out how the young balsams sprouted in enormous numbers as soon as the woods were opened up to light by the windfalls. It was rare to be hiking through my favorite woods with persons to whom each changing aspect presented questions to be answered. It was rarer to be with men whose experience and knowledge were so broad that when the facts were known, reasonable and plausible answers were forthcoming.

Some of the stands of young balsams were incredibly thick, almost like grass — still contending, still striving for individual survival. In one place they were five or six feet high and so thick they presented an impenetrable wall along the upper side of the trail.

We lunched in a sunny spot near the east limit of Mt. Sequoyah and then each of us relaxed, prone on the trail, and soaked up warmth.

We reached Tricorner Knob shelter, very neat and clean, about 3 p. m. I had told them that the Park Service trail did not climb over the top of Guyot, so George suggested that we drop our packs and hike to Guyot. This we did following the old foot trail beyond the gap. Momentarily we caught glimpses into the broad and beautiful Buck Fork, and into the headwaters of Big Creek where a post-fire growth of huckleberries was pinkly purple in the sun. The old trail was steep and we rested several times. Olaus wanted to know when we got to elevation 6580 feet, the height of the floor of Jackson Hole, Wyoming.

I had forgotten how vast was the south view from the top of Guyot — nearly 180° of it. While we were looking, a bird flew toward us, saw us, and veered sharply. Olaus said it was a falcon's flight, and deduced it must have been a duck hawk. George searched around for the highest point and stumbled onto the old bronze bench mark.

On the return we spotted a tree which had been rent by lightning. Great splinters of clean, dry wood were lying about and I picked up some for firewood. George and Olaus shouldered a piece about twelve feet long amid jibes from Dick that there was plenty of wood around the camp. But Olaus told me afterward that he had watched me look about the place for wood and was convinced it was not easy to find there. At the shelter I went to work with the little ax and soon we had a nice quick fire.

About dusk, Dick spoke of the speed of the clouds just a short distance above the tree tops. We were in bed by seven o'clock and slept the clock around. We had put spare wood under the shed and we were lucky since it was raining by morning. Breakfast was cooked in the rain.

We splashed up the trail — Dick and Zahnie far in advance, and George, Olaus, and I, behind. We stopped often to talk or pass a remark. I pointed out to George where the Ramsay Trail took off into the Greenbrier — where his brother Bob and I had climbed fifteen years earlier. Olaus in particular seemed to enjoy the fog. Near Inadu Knob I looked back and two large birds appeared out of the gloom. Olaus instantly remarked,

"Ravens," and shortly we heard them croaking after they had disappeared into the fog.

The forest on Snake Den Mountain was magnificent — virgin, all of it. Olaus asked for a photo of a tree from which the bark had been clawed by a bear. He wanted it for his Track Book.* We had descended for a couple of miles when I noticed that the spruces were unusually huge and gnarled and that we had reached the elevation of the hemlocks. The fog, shrouding those trees, as they loomed on the steep slopes below the trail, created an eerie world of matchless enchantment. Several bends of the trail brought us to a further transition zone where we saw spruce, hemlock, and pine, all near each other. The only other place I know of in the Smokies where this triple growth obtains is on the Greenbrier Pinnacle.

Rifts in the fog revealed whole mountan sides in soft, rich colors. The fog seemed to emphasize the tones. We came into the hardwoods and Olaus became interested in the leaves — chestnut, beech, gum, buckeye, magnolia, pea wood, and others, until, as he said, his head was in a whirl with the wonderful variety. He collected and took with him many specimens.

The great, shallow, gently-descending, befogged lower valley with its wooded aisles was expansive and exhilarating, although breaks in the fog would reveal sharp slopes and deeply cleft valleys across from us.

---

*Olaus Murie, *A Field Guide to Animal Tracks,*
Houghton Mifflin Company, Boston. 1954.

7

I AM BACK just four days from an eight day trip to California which concluded with a four day motor-camping trip with Dick and Doris Leonard. It was not designed to take me into really wild country, but to give me a quick look at some of the more accessible and spectacular portions of central California. I have long contended that the automobile is not designed to give one an intimate view of an area. My impressions of this trip strongly verify this. I can remember vividly only what I took in on foot when we stopped and got away from the car.

Dick gave me a brilliant description of the geology and ecology of the areas through which we passed. But my impressions are primarily my own — drawn from what I observed, and expanded slightly by the answers to questions which my own observations evoked.

We started from Berkeley. The descent into the great central valley was not as sharply etched as I had anticipated. Eventually we reached it, dry — explosively dry, straw-colored hills, and then green, irrigated fields and orchards. After crossing the San Joaquin River we moved toward the hills whose forest cover was modulated by the amount of rainfall which fell upon them. Oaks, pines, and small, understory things became greener and more luxuriant as we climbed into the zone of heavier rain.

Dick pointed out the firs and magnificent sugar pines. The limbs are almost horizontal, drooping slightly at the ends, from which, as though weighting them down, dangle the cones in their green state. There is a horizontal sweep to the limbs — broad and outreaching with those depending cones. It put me in mind of an oriental water carrier with a yoke across his shoulders and his buckets of water hanging from the ends. The bark plates of these pines, as big as the palms of one's hand, covered the boles of the tree in a bold mosaic, ruddy in the lower valleys and almost yellow higher up.

Through such a forest we were traveling by an old road, passable but occasionally washboardy. There was opportunity to see, if not to assimilate fully.

And then without warning and with no word from Doris or Dick, we came upon the big trees. I had seen the Douglas firs in the rain forest of the Olympics. I had been up the Hoh River and through the entire valley of the Bogachiel in which there were almost pure stands of those magnificent tapering firs. They were beautifully proportioned. Standing among their fellows, one was hardly aware of their size except as he might approach a trunk and measure himself alongside.

But my first impression of the *Sequoia gigantea* was so different, so staggering — tears blurred my eyes. Rising through this great mixed forest I glimpsed three russet trunks, so huge they dwarfed everything about them. In my first glimpse, they stood in the forest without root or crown, enormous, completely dominating the rest of the forest. It was as though they had been there always and that the other trees were upstarts which had grown up around them. Never had any living things been so commanding, so completely dominating.

We got out of the car at a grizzled giant — the greatest tree of them all. Paved paths led up to it. Barriers of logs were laid about it to keep people away, and to prevent the trampling of the needles through which the life-giving rains would seep. After the first glimpse I turned my back for a few moments. It was as though I were looking eternity in the face and couldn't stand it. I was suddenly confronted with the need for new values. Youth, maturity, aging, ripeness, and decline seemed not to exist. Here was Shaw's mythical race — not in the flesh, but in the form of this insouciant grove and giant. Six fathoms in diameter! A sign said this *Sequoia gigantea* had been alive for thirty-eight hundred years. Surely this was eternity. Fires it had experienced — there was evidence of that. Disease it did not know.

I sought out a lesser tree, deep in the woods, away from people. It stood breast deep in needles which had slithered down its trunk and accumulated in a soft ring about its roots. I touched the deeply furrowed bark. It was porous, velvety, and soft. I expected ruggedness, here was gentleness. One does not have to be hard when one is strong. That one tree was as old as any civilization — twice as old as the Christian era by which the western world measures its chronology.

I had my photograph taken by several of those trees. Now, I wish that I had not. I am subject to anger, passion, disease, and death. These trees seem immune to everything but life itself.

Having taken root their only destiny seems to be to live on forever. I was completely dwarfed by their all-pervasive greatness.

With typical human arrogance, roads had been built all through this grove and one loop with super-impertinence passed through a tree itself. It was not enough that people be led to one or two or a few of these trees. Some warped psychology said they must speed by all of them. There were few places where one could get completely away for his own experience with one of these trees. Throughout the entire grove automobiles, which as a species are only fifty years on this earth, buzzed about like June bugs amongst these everlasting trees. One wonders what will be the effect upon their root systems of the paving. The trees have withstood much. In their millenia they have known fire and drought. For twenty years now they have known cars and roads. Will they survive this intrusion with the same sublime aloofness? One wishes heartily that the administrators, the men who decree the roads, had absorbed some of the divine unconcern of these trees and had left them their peace.

We walked about, just why I am not sure except that it is the nature of men to walk about. I was glad to observe that young trees are springing up, and that this is no passing phenomenon. The trees seem to grow as well on slopes as in moist swales. I did not get over the surprise of having my entire view blocked by one of these giants as I walked close by. One does not get close to these trees and come away the same.

But back to the Sierra. In the darkness we hunted out the campground. No one was there but us. Heavy Jeffrey pines ringed about us and the stars were infinite, bright, and unblinking. The wind soughed through the branches. It was the same theme which all pines play, sad and untouchable. Only here the orchestration was different. These were heavier pines than I had known, with heavier needles. There was more volume to the music but the same haunting aloofness.

There had been lightning along our route to this place. Although I had wondered, one does not like to make brash inquiries when in the mountain domain of others. But as though reading my unspoken question, Dick had said,

"It never rains in the Sierras at night."

I was content therefore to lay out my mattress and spread my sleeping bag under the open sky. The sky never became completely overcast. But as night wore on there was a blurring of the stars and an ominous spatter of rain. Dick got up and returned with tents which he spread over us to ward off the wet. Actually it never rained. There were always portions of the sky which were bright with stars. For one who has lived for nearly four decades with the unpredictable Smokies, the incident is hardly worth mentioning. But since so much had been promised in California, by rights that splash of rain should be noted!

At the first suggestion of dawn, I arose and took in several overlooks to the east as I walked to the edge of the valley. Half Dome, even in the half light of the pre-dawn, dominated the scene as completely as the great sequoias had dominated the forest the afternoon before. In the gray dawn-light, the soft high-lighting of the plunging, rounding slope seized the senses. No photograph I have seen begins to portray the monstrous bulk of this great rock mass. It is inescapable. One's eyes stray but come back inevitably to that precipitous south slope.

There was little warmth in the view – rather something

austere and distant. But it was grandeur on an incomparable scale. Beyond Half Dome and rising high in the east were the high Sierras. From their mountain meadows and snow fields, water gathered and funneled into Nevada Falls and then into the clean-plunging Vernal Falls. Standing there alone I heard a kind of dry, horny knocking, like a wagon going over the loose boards of a bridge in the Smokies. The Leonards later spoke of this as the "rockets," caused by great masses or chunks of water breaking loose in the fall and rocketing against the lower slope.

Dawn was memorable with high serrated peaks, ominous, heavy clouds, vast distances and that potent, terrifying slope of Half Dome. Even as we walked back through the woods its curve broke the skyline as something cold and awesome and different.

After breakfast we went to Sentinel Dome where at the very top a lone twisted pine had crowded its roots into a crack and had hung on. Its presence relieved the summit of Sentinel Dome as there had been nothing to relieve the solid, enormous bulk and lines and curves of Half Dome. I could not understand why it actually was half a dome. Could the glacier which came down the valley have scraped off the other half? Dick said no. That flat line was apparently one of the joints of the bedding plane and it had become thrust upward into that position.

The rounded slopes are characteristic of granite mountains, as I am well aware from the same general outlines of Looking Glass Rock and Whitesides in North Carolina, and of course Stone Mountain in Georgia. These eastern mountains are much darker in color, due probably to the heavier growth of lichens.

Dick called my attention to the signs which rock climbers read. A darker color in the rock usually indicates water and lichens. Perfectly white or grayer rock beneath betokens an

52

overhang from which the water drops leaving the under part free of lichens. Vertical or near vertical striping on the surface of these domes may mark the course of rock falls, as well as the path of water. He showed me the crumbling and crunching in the rock faces where the glaciers had ground against them. He also showed me and I felt with my finger tips the smoothness of "glacial polish." This "polish," according to François Matthes, is not so much a manifestation of a glacier's power, as of its frustration.

Leaving Sentinel Dome we drove around a promontory and down into Yosemite Valley itself. Someone has called it "The Incomparable Valley." Incomparable in its giant, stupendous faces. Incomparable in its challenge to the new race of rock climbers. Incomparable in its lunging waterfalls. But far from incomparable — rather ordinary in its crowding; in its tasteless buildings; in the yielding to use of its once lovely meadows.

We left this behind and took again to the heights with Tuolumne Meadows as our objective. Part of this trip was along a new road in beautiful forest. In country which was rolling enough to lend itself to unique treatment, this road in many spots was as straight and rigid as a slide rule. Alongside we saw young firs with their branches sprawled and flared and shallowly cupped.

Part of our route, about twenty miles of it, then lay along the old Tioga mining road. In many places it was one-laned, abrupt, and erratic in its grade and wound intimately and narrowly through the forest. One traveled it slowly, and as much as one can from a car we got the feel of the forest, because we were traveling slowly and alertly, as the road demanded. Road courtesy came into being and was uniformly practiced. The up-car had the right of way and the down-car would pull aside to give it headway. Greetings and acknowledgments were exchanged. Here was camaraderie along the road, something almost unique in this day of modern high-speed highways. Have we gained or have we lost? Have we substituted a blur for rich and sharp impressions of persons and things? It takes experience of the wilderness even to raise these questions, a function of wilderness which should be emphasized.

We were getting higher in the Sierras. Vegetation, trees became more sparse; bare granite, more abundant; the occasional lake, more lovely. We came at last to a great straw-colored flat — Tuolumne Meadows. Three weeks before it had been green, they said. Now it was seared by frost. Its austere and lovely bleakness appealed to me deeply. Its wide spaciousness expanded my soul. We camped on a stony projecting rib amongst a few trees. I listened to the wind in the trees. Again the melody was the same. We sat out under the stars with a curved log at our backs. A cold wind fingered our necks. The stars were brilliant and unblinking above us. There was no one else around. Here was the beginning of wilderness.

At the dawn, I dressed warmly and followed the rocky promontory to the flats, and the flats to the river. A transparent mist clung like a blanket to the wide-reaching meadows. I felt a suspicious whiteness on the bridge. It was frost. Across the meadows and rising sharply and bleakly above me were jagged, naked peaks with talus all around and terrifying slopes and points. Here was the real "high country," which I was destined on this trip to view from below. For the most part the sky was clear, but in a low divide to the east wind-blown clouds clung without moving and caught the fairy colors of the oncoming

55

sun. Rose at first and then brilliant, dazzling, golden yellow. Unicorn Peak back of me picked up the light, and the band of shadows dropped lower. Trees on a slope behind me became resplendent and the sky burned with a dazzling light around a pyramid to the east. Then so quickly, it seemed the earth must have lunged downward to meet the sun, the meadow was bright with light and the blanketing mist vanished. As though purposing to overwhelm me Doris and Dick had taken me first to the groves, then to the peaks, and now had brought me a sunrise from a mountain meadow.

At Tioga Pass we were in alpine country. There were yet a few trees, including the whitebark pine of timber line; but essentially there were the clean-lined tundra effects with diminutive flowers, gentians as tiny and shy as violets, or our mountain iris at home. The lake was cold and immaculate and was ringed with rocks. Above were gaunt, rocky peaks and slides. There was little confusion — here the struggle for life was so dramatic, so obvious . . .

ADIRONDACKS

On our trip to the Adirondacks I heard the winds in many places. I became aware of something which I had experienced but which had really not registered with me before — the vast differences in the sound of the wind passing through different types of trees. At Fahnestock Park, where there was a preponderance of hemlocks, there was a soft, ethereal quality to it — not too soft to hear — but too soft to analyze and, oh, so sweet to the human spirit.

There was a roaring power to it in the mixed forest along the Sacandaga River in the southern Adirondacks. There was nothing delicate about it; it was full-throated, with a surge that stirred me excitedly. I repeat, I had not been aware in my mind of the vast differences in the sound of the wind. I can not distinguish now in my mind the subtleties of the wind in the spruce and fir forests of Mt. Colvin and in the vast cathedral-like groves of the white pines in Cook Forest in Pennsylvania.

There was a subtlety to the sound of the wind in both forests. There was an elusive continuousness, rising and falling in volume but never ceasing, which is like no sound on earth. There is sadness in it for me, even as it stirs me deeply. I don't know why it should sadden me, except that it is more tentative, less tangible, than the music of any orchestra. The needles — the prime sources of the music — are myriad and fragile and yet the whole air is pervaded and overwhelmed with this light thrumming which has no beginning or ending. I can not compass it any more than I can compass life itself.

8

JACKSON HOLE
YELLOWSTONE NATIONAL PARK
WYOMING
SUN RIVER
BOB MARSHALL WILDERNESS AREA
MONTANA
1953

I N LESS than twenty-four hours we were whisked from the heavy heat and my work at Oak Ridge to the bracing air and clean simplicities of the Murie Ranch in Jackson Hole, Wyoming. Stimulated by the air and the Council members who were assembling at the ranch, I got up just after dawn and blowed off into the woods alone. The sun had already turned the Teton range a dazzling gray and white. I picked up an animal trail and followed it to a swampy slough. A dark form moved behind some trees. It was a moose. He had heard me and had his ears alerted. The water was moving slowly. Across from me was the range. Before me was this grand wild creature; dark, pure, flowing water; a kingfisher diving into it; and an osprey. Here was sweet simplicity.

* * * * * * * * * * *

We are back in Knoxville from our trip west. As usual, I found no time to make any notes. All of the record of the trip is in my mind and heart.

I rock-climbed with Dick Leonard; worked up through a break in the Chinese Wall largely on my own, and walked the seventeen miles from Gates Park to Klick Brothers ranch. I chopped wood, got up at dawn nearly every morning to see what I could of wildlife, and learned what Eric Shipton meant when he said that after a few weeks of strenuous physical activity one becomes tremendously fit.

All of these things point up the vast gap between the lives most of us live and the marvelous, serene experiences to which we treated ourselves on the trip. I am convinced there was not one of us who participated in The Wilderness Society Council meeting and field trip who wanted to come back from that rosy comradeship to civilization's demands; and yet there was not one of us, including Olaus Murie and Sig Olson, who did not feel strongly the tug to get back to the busy world each had left. Bob Marshall once said, so far as personal preference went, he would have made his home in Alaska, but he felt he should live in the lower States where the problems were.

And so, most of us are now back at our tasks which are performed in an atmosphere and environment which many of us but tolerate. What can we do to re-enrich those environments? What have we really learned from our trip?

59

YELLOWSTONE

The area around Old Faithful in Yellowstone Park has become so built up that one has difficulty finding his way about. A ranger with a microphone and loudspeaker gave the story of the geysers and talked while Old Faithful worked up to an eruption. The atmosphere was holidayish but there was no wilderness. There was display without a strong personal impact. Even so, one church, playing upon the great popular curiosity about Old Faithful, announced that its services were adjusted to Old Faithful's eruptions. There seemed a curious, if humorous, honesty in that sign — a suggestion that a personal experience with the realities of the universe is more important than more ceremonious observances.

Later in the evening we drove over to the campground at the Madison entrance and stopped en route at many of the other geysers and hot springs. The civilized gloss that surrounded Old Faithful had not affected these and I wondered deeply at the violent heat which was present only a few feet below the surface, and which resulted in these guttural rushings of steam and of water and mud. This had been going on for thousands of years. What must have been the reactions of the early explorers who without warning saw them for the first time. In late dusk we looked down one valley from a slight eminence. Scores of plumes of steam rose lazily in the cool air. A substantial stream of fresh water twisted along the surface of the earth catching reflections of the steam and the gorgeous green and yellow after-glow of the sunset. All the boiling turbulence of the pools and vents was far from us; the milling crowds of people had hunted out their havens for the night, leaving us alone with this haunting and lovely scene.

Around the springs and geysers mosquitoes swarmed thickly. I suppose they were attracted by the warmth, for we found out later that their activity was always reduced as the air chilled.

The climax of that evening came unexpectedly. We had stopped to examine another pool. It was almost dark. There was little we could see as we padded the footboards which the Park Service had laid over the crumbling and seething earth. We could feel the thin barbs of the mosquitoes as they pierced two and three layers of clothing. None but us was around the springs. Then out of the silence of the night there came a weird, high cry.

"Coyotes," Dick said.

The cry rose and fell, high and unearthly and was answered from down the valley. Then silence. It was so unbelievable, we strained to hear it again. But as inscrutably as it began, it ceased and we were left with but a tingling memory. Some say the world would be better off if the coyotes were killed off and that cry forever stilled. I dissent.

The next morning we saw an enormous bull bison chewing contentedly at the grass. People swarmed from their cars to see the buffalo, as though they were starved for the sight of something old and natural and primordial. And yet, so far have we moved from that past, several nearly grown boys referred to the bison as a deer. It crossed the road and we watched it climb the steep cut on the far side. Its shoulders were enormous, sloping steeply upward from comparatively low and small hips. As it lunged up the slope it seemed to climb with its front legs and scotch itself with its back legs. These latter seemed too frail for their task, and once it looked as though they would collapse completely before the forelegs could reach for further footing. Once these great creatures were numbered in the millions. Today, there are a few thousand in reservations but not too many are found in the back country. So completely has our agricultural-industrial culture blanketed the land, only a lucky few people ever see a buffalo.

Yellowstone Park is many things, including a huge rolling upland of lodgepole pine. Its chief features are its animals, its thermal manifestations, its lake and falls. We saw bear, bison, coyote, and deer in surroundings which were not indigenous. We ate and camped with hordes of people. They were decent, orderly, and interested in their land. It seemed not to bother too many that the sight of Old Faithful, the Mammoth Hot Spring, and the bison were not segregated from the world of roads and automobiles.

SUN RIVER COUNTRY

As we drove north from Helena, Montana, we passed through beautiful, green, rolling grasslands. In the background, on either side were mountains, and the earth was delicately toned by wild flowers — roses, lupine, calendulas, and flax. There was never anything more subtly exquisite than those streamers and splotches of lavender and yellow catching the eye everywhere through the grassland.

At Camp McDonald Dick invited me to climb the cliff to the west. I was both loathe and eager. I had never been on rock. I did not know how my nerves would hold up. But I wanted to find out and I had complete confidence in him. We took rope, pitons, carabiners, a hammer, and a small pack with cameras, etc. I could not question the taking of pitons, since it was his trip. After I got on the rock face, I did not question their use.

We scrambled up the scree to the foot of the cliff and reckoned we had eight hundred feet of rock face to climb. Dick gave me the choice of a relatively easy route with a good chance of reaching the top or a harder route with less chance. I chose the former because of my untried nerves. He started up and soon reached a belaying point. I started up. The rock was limestone, and was sharp and heavily fractured. I had not gotten ten feet above the scree before my nerves became tense.

Dick took infinite pains. But the lead man is very much on his own. The rope protects him from a disastrous fall but not from a dangling slip with much bruising. Once, as I moved toward Dick, a chunk of rock pulled loose under my right hand. Dick laughed and said,

"That is embarrassing."

He showed me how to pull against two projections with my arms outstretched in such a way as to support my whole body. He drove in a piton. It broke loose. He tried another crack, and left the hammer for me to remove it. For a half hour, I supplied a belay from behind a small juniper. Finally he told me to come on. The rope stretched across a bulge of bare rock. I could not see him. I was on my own. He pulled the rope until I felt it snugly against my waist. It was a great comfort. I glanced down fifty feet of bare, steeply pitched rock to the scree. It might as well have been a thousand.

But I couldn't go. Handholds were non-existent. Dick said the footholds were better than they looked. Was a shelf of rock, half the size of my hand, tilted steeply downward, better than it looked? This I doubted. I thought of another route, but the rope went through a carabiner. I was bound to that route or

63

must give up the rope. I sweated — became slightly panicky. There were no footholds, no usable handholds. I was stuck and disgraced. Finally, Dick said,

"The rope will support you; use it to climb with."

I started out with a strong sense of its protection. Those down-pitched knobs of rock held, unbelievably. I moved quickly and confidently across that appalling spot with almost no help from Dick and soon joined him on a secure ledge behind a tree. It was one of the greatest moments of my life. I found that at 51 I had the nerve for rock climbing. We had taken two hours to climb one hundred feet.

We decided to go back by a shelving ledge which was relatively easy, except for loose rock which we pulled away from the cliff in great rotten chunks. Actually at that point my nerves were relaxed. The worst spots had occurred on the up-climb on bare faces which had terrifyingly small and down-pitched hand and footholds.

On Tuesday evening we went for a barbecue on the winter range which had been recently acquired by the State of Montana for the elk which summered back in the Bob Marshall Wilderness area. It was high upland prairie, which piled in huge rounded heavings against old Saw Tooth and its foothills. The grass was luxuriant and deep, and softly colored with wild flowers. We climbed a knoll where there were some pines. We stirred up a deer and fawn and came to a high overlook whence we could see reservoirs and the flat, grassy prairie. Finally we came to the place of the barbecue where a number of wilderness-minded sportsmen joined us for the meal and an evening of talk.

64

The site was high. The earlier vistas and the upsweep of the mixed grass and forest lands to the mountains created a sense of immense distances. A large campfire was lighted about which we sat for warmth. Back of me the pale orange-green alpenglow, spreading upward from the black outline of the mountains, held my eyes. It was beautiful and lingered for hours after the sun had set, as though it could not bear to leave the serene perfection of the scene. As the men talked, I could hear the wind gently touching the trees which came down from the mountains in long fingers of growth. The breeze was barely audible, emanating in thin waves of sound out of space.

I left the campfire and walked back through that airy sound toward the afterglow. The campfire lit the faces and bodies of those gathered about it. Their voices carried above the gentle sigh of the wind to the spot where I stood. The fire and people were an infinitely small part of the vast dim scene of plain and mountain. I watched for a few moments. And I was stricken with a kind of fright. Here was magnificent beauty and peace. People like these tiny figures around this campfire had fought for this beautiful range. Others, in greater numbers, had burned our forests, had denuded our plains, had extinguished noble species of game, had muddied our rivers, and were sweeping the richness of our country to the oceans and the Gulf. Never had the mad, irresponsible power of mankind been so impressed upon me. Pressed by an unmatured, temporal philosophy, these creatures, bewilderingly small like those around the campfire, had moved devastatingly westward across the plains. Around the fire were men who loved the peace and beauty of their earth. They loved the animals, the range, the space, and the freedom. What the wilderness movement needs to do more than anything else is to reinstate, or perhaps bring to people generally for the first time the same love and reverence for the natural scene. It would seem to be an optimum goal for all mankind. Nominally accepted, population and resources, natural beauty, and human serenity and sanity would have full play. Man would move worthily across the earth and the earth would bloom and blossom as we had seen it on the way to this place.

BOB MARSHALL WILDERNESS AREA

On Wednesday we left Camp McDonald in a truck for the wilderness pack trip. We lurched over a hot, dusty road to Lake Gibson and there boarded a boat for the trip to the foot of Sun Butte. This was a steep, craggy peak, carrying a reef of black rocks, which would be one anchor for the proposed Sun Butte dam on the North Fork. Reaching the summit, we saw wild sheep across from us. But the extraordinary view was of the great park-like meadows extending in light green stretches long distances upstream between the mountains. Such amplitude, such inviting spaciousness, such richness in this juncture of plain and mountain! It was the first visit of James and George Marshall to the wilderness area which had been named for their brother Bob.

Later we followed those meadows. Bernie Frank and I set out on foot. At first the turf seemed thin and overgrazed. But as we progressed the grass deepened, as did my love for these great open plains and uplands of grass. Here were distances, splendid and beyond description, where time and progress were slowed to a walk. This was wilderness with a boundless landscape where persons on foot or horse were mere specks upon the earth.

The meadows followed the river but their flanks climbed

the lower slopes of the mountains. Aspen copses darkened and splotched them and evergreens drifted down tentatively from the higher slopes. Lupine and flax were in bloom. Everything was so perfect one lost the sense of being deep in wilderness. Later we were to find one or two cabins, an incongruous telephone line, an emergency landing strip, and bridges where such things ought not to be. But these things had not done great damage and they could easily be removed or abandoned.

We camped the first night at Cabin Creek, where we cooked with wood and drew water from a swirling stream nearby. Downstream a few rods, beavers had laid a dam fifty yards long and had built a house in the middle of the pool. We slept under a fringe of trees amidst swarming mosquitoes. Surprisingly enough, Anne and I, who had often combated eastern gnats, were hardly bothered by them, although others spoke the next morning of fighting them off during the night.

Bob Cooney took us by a lick the next morning — a great, bare, trampled saucer of a place. No animals, but in the afternoon, as I was walking with Olaus and Bernie along another of those great untended meadows, our eyes were arrested by a movement on a grassy eminence a mile away. Looking closer we saw a flowing, tawny stream of animals. Made up of individuals it seemed to have the cohesion of something fluid. It was elk — fifty of them. We paused and watched, and back of us others paused and watched this marvelous wild spectacle. The elk were milling and galloping, in a curious, effortless gliding movement.

We had now made the connection between the winter range we had visited two evenings before and the summer range. Here the elk were on the abundant grasslands of this remote and seemingly boundless valley. This was not the full picture. Up under the Continental Divide there were many narrow side valleys which swelled at the end into bulb-like alpine meadows where there were smaller herds.

On this second day out we finally came to the wide and swift-flowing North Fork (of the Sun River). So wide and ample was the main valley, we had been paralleling the river for nearly two days without having seen it. This unbarriered space was exhilarating. One could walk, walk, walk for seemingly endless distances with little sign of man. The trails were mostly game trails — the range was natural and the animals wild. There was no economy here except the economy of nature. Of course man had tinkered with it a bit. But here were multitudes and many species of game animals. We saw signs of them all — elk, deer, mountain sheep, mountain goats, black bear, grizzlies, coyotes, cougars, and wolves. Here in wild balance was the kind of wilderness people were seeking. It was tremendous, exquisite, infinitely appealing and provocative.

Gates Park seemed large when we were in it. From the side of Baretop Mountain two days later it appeared a mere sliver of light green in a deep forested saucer of mountains. It was a grassy park on a side stream and was spotted with the yellow potentilla. There were a lake, three or four cabins, a corral, the landing strip, and a fenced run for horses. But all around were forest, bogs, and mountains not too far away. We had passed the last rampart and were in the inner citadel of the wilderness, with the Chinese Wall not far to the west of us. But twenty people bring with them some of the influences of civilization. The horses had to be taken care of; there was bathing in the creek; tents were erected and food was cooked.

Some of us walked over near the salt lick and sat for an hour on a little rise above the lake in the long twilight of the north and fought mosquitoes and watched deer.

It was thought that it would be damp in the flat of the valley. So Anne and I carried our packs and sleeping bags to a little knoll which jutted out between the cabins and the lake. Although the mosquitoes had not seriously disturbed us, we thought they might be less vigorous on the knoll.

We lay on the ground. There was a magnificent golden-green alpenglow up-valley from us. It seemed it should be in the west, but John Craighead's compass and the pointers of the Big Dipper showed it to be in the north. The chill of the night abated the mosquitoes. The next morning even in dry air our sleeping bags were slightly dampened and frosted.

In this remote, beautiful, and somewhat gentle scene we had slept. Drowsing in the early dawn, I snapped to attention. Out of pure space, filling the valley and echoing and reechoing through its confines, was a wild, high-pitched wail as involved and eerie as a skirl from Scottish bagpipes. It overlapped and pulsated, not blood-curdling and frightening, but high and shrill with a baffling, irrepressible quality, which concluded with three high-pitched barks ending in a kind of scream, as though the creatures responsible were trying to pump further life into this wilderness ululation. Coyotes!

Elsewhere I have written that the tinkling notes of the winter wren seem to vitalize the Smoky Mountains. Here the curling cries of the coyotes seemed to epitomize this scene. Up to that moment, I had felt somewhat at home in this eastern edge of the Bob Marshall Wilderness. We had hiked hard through its glorious open meadows. But everything seemed open, obvious. The spicey society of like-minded friends gave it a familiarity. And then this wailing prelude to the dawn upended my mood. I capitulated humbly to the real denizens of this place. I was only a visitor and felt my frustration. What could these creatures have been about as they broke open the dawn with their cries? What secrets of the present — what secrets of an immeasurable past were woven into this shrill undulating cry? I was no more at home in their world than I would have been on Times Square. Could anyone ever fathom the secrets of this howling-barking?

When I woke her, Anne sat bolt upright in her sleeping bag and listened. When the rolling cries no longer echoed from the hills, she turned to me with luminous smile. At that moment, I realized for the first time in our lives we had broken the real boundaries of civilization and were brushing shoulders with the wilderness.

Wildness needs great space. Already I was seeing how far the elk must migrate between their summer and winter ranges in order to preserve their existence. Already man had brought trails and wires and cabins and bridges into this land of the elk and coyote. Fine as it was, it could be finer and purer. Man in addition to sustenance needs unalloyed space and these unalloyed experiences. I felt grateful for the expansive vision of Bob Marshall who had preached the doctrine of wilderness to the musty, cloistered minds of the administrators. I felt thankful for the contagion of his spirit which had overrun lethargy and opposition in the Forest and Indian Services and had resulted in the sequestration of so many such areas. Can we who follow protect these spaces and wild creatures from greed and short-sightedness and from increasing population and business pressures? We must by every means at our command sell wilderness to the world as surely as the coyotes sold it to me that morning.

Three mornings in succession we were awakened deep in the inexpressible half light of dawn by these soft yet shrill, pulsing cries.

The next day we went up Red Shale Creek through gently ascending forests to the alpine meadow at the foot of the talus and cliffs of broken rock of the Continental Divide. En route we had to chop out blowdowns across the trail, and Olaus, reading the wilderness "newspaper," found that a grizzly had been coming down-trail toward us less than two hours before. Along the trail were orchises and columbine and lilies, shy and lovely; and on the red dome of Red Shale Mountain we saw through binoculars the tiny, sunlit bodies of mountain goats.

I have been in alpine meadows before but never so far from a roadhead. There was a special charm here — grass and evergreens and snow banks and scree and rushing streams were thrown together in charming proximity under the wall-like crest of the Continental Divide. Here there were avalanche lilies similar to the trout lilies of the Smokies but without their mottled leaf, and many other flowers of early spring. Each finger of a snow bank terminated in rivulets which shimmered through the grass, and merged finally in crystal-clear ice-cold streams. In a side opening in the valley, behind a screen of spruces, someone spotted a herd of elk and half the party stalked them in the hope of a better view.

But I wanted to go higher and broke away from the crowd to a snow slope up which I toiled toward the trail which angled upward across the scree. I intercepted it just behind Bob Cooney and just ahead of Anne. The three of us saw a fine elk not a hundred feet away through the trees.

But the wall tempted me. I saw a break in it. A great gendarme stood alone and back of it a cleft which, though obscure, might lead to the top. I started directly for the gendarme and quickly found myself in the middle of a slope of

71

small scree which was barely in repose. Below the scree was a drop of twenty feet. No game trail furnished footing across this, as on Sheep Mountain five years before, and ignominiously and with infinite care, I inched backward and downward to an outcrop of firm rock and safety.

Anne decided she wanted none even of the firm rock and went down to join Olaus at the lake.

I tried again on heavy talus and made good progress. Bob Cooney and John Craighead were now ahead of me; George Marshall and Bernie Frank, just behind. Bob was well up in the cleft, motionless and dark against the light rock.

We were in a crumbled cleft in the Chinese Wall, an eye-catching stratification of limestone which marks the Continental Divide for a distance of nearly thirty miles. I have wondered in my mind whether the man who named it the Chinese Wall was viewing it at the time from a distance, or from up close. From a distance it was a distinctly stratified, undulatory, almost vertical wall of rock topped off with cornices of snow. Up close, it was not only richly stratified horizontally, but also highly fractured vertically. In the cleft and elsewhere, it was as unstable as a wall laid up dry and without mortar. Climbing that cleft after one got above the talus was like climbing a wall of loose, unanchored stones which had been partially dislodged from position. There were several small ledges, and openings between the stones, which from below seemed to offer numerous hand and footholds.

Close up, it was a terrifying pile of unstable stones so tenuously piled that we hardly dared touch one for fear of dislodging it. I watched Bob and John. They moved with infinite care. Once I shrank back in a cavity as John, affrighted, dislodged a chunk of rock as big as a coffee table. He had seized

hold of it only to have it come free under his weight. It pinwheeled down by me and between George and Bernie. I watched with worried fascination as it struck a huge stone in the talus and exploded into a hundred pieces.

Once I was just beneath John as he unintentionally dislodged another stone. I looked up just in time to catch it crashing against the underside of my forearm. After that we proceeded one at a time. One spot in the cleft worried me. I could find no foothold. Then I laid a knee on a shelf, wedged myself, and passed that spot. I was near the top. Bob and John were watching and warned me against a chimney, advising me to follow a steeply-pitched shelf of unsecured stones. I was still mindful of that uncertain experience down on the scree slope, and chose the chimney. Extending my body between shoulders and boots, I wedged my way up and came out on top.

This was the great Continental Divide. It was flat mountain tundra overlying horizontal strata of rock. Alpine flowers bloomed at surface level. I looked west. The top was plateau-like perhaps two or three hundred yards across. On it were patches of snow, tongues of forest, and areas of rock spotted brilliantly with creeping alpine flowers. Beyond the plateau was a jumbled mass of peaks which Bob said reached to the western edge of the Bob Marshall Wilderness area.

We started south at a breath-taking walk. As I recall, the elevation was about eight thousand feet. I recall Bob Cooney saying he would "walk clear to Mexico, if necessary," rather than go back down the cleft! He seemed to know of another break in the wall. We plowed across a snow field, wormed through thickets of dwarfed timber, and padded across sun-baked rocks. Always the snow or rock looked ominously steep to the east. We did not dare venture close to those overhanging cornices of snow.

Eventually the top dipped into a shallow saddle and we ventured a look. Leading off the crest was a snow slope and in its center was an elk trail which continued down a buttressing ridge which marked the south boundary of the little valley where we had lunched. Remembering our experience on Sheep Mountain, I felt relieved the minute I saw the animal trail. Wherever the elk trail went, we could follow it, I felt, and would eventually get down.

We looked down into the next valley south and saw elk. There in a grassy park, surrounded and interspersed by firs in as fair a scene as I ever saw, were twenty of those stately animals completely at ease and undisturbed. Several were lying down, relaxed, and unalerted. It was a peaceful and idyllic scene which reflected the vast extent and remoteness of the area. As I gazed down at them, the scene was so utterly natural, so devoid of man's meddling influences I was moved to say to Bob,

"Almost I would become a grass-eater just to live in such a place of perfection."

We had no trouble on the ridge. We called to friends at the lunch site and eventually heard a hail back of us. It was John Craighead inquiring how to leave the wall. He looked tiny and forlorn, outlined against the sky. While Bob shouted directions to him, I found where the elk had cut back off the ridge onto the main slope. Bob said he could go anywhere an elk could go, but it was not until we found fresh elk tracks, that we left the ridge. The going was safe enough until we intercepted some prodigiously steep snow fields. Bob hit these almost at once; and after a tentative try or two, down I went at a terrific pace, crazily maintaining my equilibrium as I took giant striding steps downward. I came to water. I was dehydrated and drank cup after cup of freshly melted snow. It rested cold in my stomach. By now the exhilaration was so great, I unwittingly sped on past the spot where the horses were tied.

Meanwhile, George and Bernie had decided the cleft was too dangerous and had not tried to reach the top. Dick, Doris, and Zahnie had climbed a scree slope short of the gendarme and traveled roped up, moving one at a time, to the foot of the wall. Olaus and Anne witnessed all ascents from the lake.

9

HOW HARD it is to turn from the perfections of this October day in East Tennessee to the events and anxieties of the last month. We were in magnificent country in New Mexico — remote and inviting. Gaunt cliffs walled in glorious canyons. Great trees sprang from moist valleys and clear streams flowed from the vastnesses above. And yet many of the areas we visited are under fire from profit-minded citizens who would swap the silences and serenities of the natural woods for more automobiles, more pacing, more noise, more uniformity. In few places did we find stability of thinking and philosophy. Wilderness is under scrutiny, if not under attack, in many of the places we went.

The battle is joined — not for particular parks or monuments in forests or wilderness areas but for a philosophy of land use. Congressman George Miller of California has said that no lands will persist unexploited unless they are deliberately set aside and protected, and unless there is faithfulness in respecting those dedications.

The Wilderness Society Council is concerned about ways and means to reach people who are not allied with our cause. Perhaps we should make inquiry amongst the fifty or sixty million visitors to the national parks. How did they get interested? How were they inspired to go? Was it because of the lack in their everyday environment, a lack which was summed up by one of the women at the Trail Riders' meeting in Santa Fe? When asked why she joined the Trail Riders, she said she came to see some trees, commenting that she always liked the night in the treeless prairie where she lived, because then she "couldn't see the things that are not there." I wonder if that is what national park and national forest visitors miss in their home environments, the subtle lack of things that are not there, things which their instinct tells them should be there.

PECOS WILDERNESS

What did we see that *was* there? Our first trip was into the southeast corner of the Pecos Wilderness area — to a canyon which was a kind of an adjunct of the main Pecos divide. The walls were a thousand feet high, fluted and yellow and brown in color. Their crumbling sides rolled out into the canyon floor in several places, encroaching almost upon the stream itself. The water was clear and cool, with a warm overtone from the colored rocks over which it flowed. There were occasional grassy meadows, tiny things surrounded by spruces and firs.

We went by a small ravine and a cleft in the canyon wall to

Hermit Peak, the high point on the outside wing of the canyon, and the last rampart of mountains. Hermit Peak was rather sparsely forested, a broad, flat mountain a half mile in length. Beyond it to the east were declining foothills and the plains of New Mexico, Oklahoma, and Texas. It was a highly dramatic place with stupendous views into the subdued eastern country, and west into the still wild mountains.

One of the memorable things about the trip was a rain and sleet storm. There had been lightning and growls of thunder, and the storm broke just as we descended under beetling cliffs the steepest and roughest part of the trail. My horse had been almost frantic for water at a stone well-spring on top. There were so many horses to be watered and the water was so limited, that I persuaded him to go on down the trail until we would hit the stream.

The storm, a very chilling one, struck before we reached the stream. Water poured in a thin cascade from the cliffs and gathered in the trail. This water was brown and murky from the dust that was mixed with it, and yet my horse tried to drink out of the trail. I would have permitted it, but Don Clauser, the leader, said rather roughly,

"Don't let him drink that."

I rode on, getting colder and colder, until we came to the thin thread of the creek which hardly had more water in it than the trail higher up. My horse pushed in under the trees and undergrowth and drank and drank and drank from small puddles, sucking them dry many times and waiting for them to fill up again.

79

GILA WILDERNESS

The next day we drove back to Albuquerque and joined forces again with the Franks and George and Zahnie. We set off down through hot, dry, desert country, paralleling the green sabre of the Rio Grande, toward the tiny village of Datil, New Mexico. There we would turn off through spreading plain and mesa country toward the eastern edge of the Gila forest. It was after dark before we left Datil and we did not see the magnificence of this intervening country until our return ten days later.

From Datil to the Slater cabin we were on a maze of dirt roads in country not too well mapped, and entirely unfamiliar to any of us. We were in the second car. At each intersection the lead car would stop. The dome light would flick on and a little tableau with Bernie and Zahnie as chief participants would be enacted again and again. Bernie, intense and earnest, would study his maps and Zahnie would look on, like a big German burgomaster. Then an argument would ensue with much gesticulation by Bernie and calm, judicial expostulation by Zahnie. Then to another intersection where it would all be repeated. Once they stopped where there was no road. Bernie went out into the woods with his flashlight and George walked back with a big grin on his face:

"The Continental Divide," he said.

Finally we intersected a road which seemed to be properly oriented with the Continental Divide. We turned on to this, dodged some boulders, ploughed through two sloughs and were at our destination.

We arrived about 9:30 p.m. I, who have been conditioned in the damp and rainy Smokies, looked at the cabin. But Dick who has been conditioned in the dry and, most times, rainless Sierras went out under the towering pines. It was my first experience with the ponderosas. He called me to a level bench near a grouping of three or four of these massive trees. There was a cushion of needles under them and a few cones and dry faggots. Here four of us bedded down − Dick and Doris a little below; Anne and I at the foot of one of the great trees.

As we settled for the night, I became aware of something upon which I have been on the threshold in the Smokies, but never experienced − unbroken stillness. There were no birds calling − no air stirring − no falling cones − and everybody was far enough away I could not hear their breathing. Silence − the great silence of the earth and of the cosmos! Under those mighty trees, in the still, cool light of a near-full moon, it was breath-taking. I was transported by the wonder and beauty of it. As I once thought in the Smokies − how could such enormous manifestations of life, be so completely at rest.

As long as I live, I shall never forget those hours of silence. It was as though all the concentrated noises of living had suddenly been spirited away, leaving only that vibrant silence. There was no vacuum, no sterility to it, rather like the quiet beginnings of all life.

A week later and still in the Gila Wilderness Anne and I took a trip on foot down White Creek from the ranger's cabin. We were told of a horseshoe curve in the creek about five miles down, which was boxed in by cliffs and very spectacular. We started out in the heart of the valley and almost immediately had to ford the creek. The trail climbed rapidly onto ledges of volcanic rock, and we looked down into the creek where it was forced between deep massive ledges in a kind of millrace. There were one or two little cascades and some nice pools. In the afternoon as we returned, we saw a water ouzel on the smooth rock beside one of the cascades. We watched it for many minutes as it stood in the sheeting water, ducking its head, completely submerging itself and throwing the spray of water far behind. It always faced upstream and seemed to have an uncanny knack of holding its footing in swift water. Its feathers were so oily that it came out of each bath without the slightest sign of drenching. It is a fascinating bird, a life study in itself.

Our path mounted higher on the cliffs. The gravel rolled loosely and insecurely under our feet. We began to work out of the moist gloom of the valley into the scorching sunlight. This I did not like. The undergrowth did not seem to be too dense along the creek, so we decided to take potluck, as we would have done in the Smokies. The going was easier. Wherever we had to cross the stream, there were stones or boulders and we managed to cross dry shod. I don't remember too much about the vegetation. A few places along the creek there were thickets of willows. But much of the time the going was through open woods of ponderosa pine. We lunched beside a long pool of clear water which flowed alongside a naked ledge. There was not as much undergrowth and the rock was different, since nearly everything was volcanic here. But otherwise in this moist canyon we were reminded of the Smokies. Of course we do not in the Smokies have the great yellow and almond-colored perpendicular cliffs on the edges of our valleys. Our cliffs are gray and rounded and marked with lichens. Nor are our game trails as well defined.

On the return, we followed what I took to be a deer trail

most of the way, and by so doing we avoided crossing the creek. I think we were both a little disappointed that we saw no rattlesnakes, about which we had been warned. And we were both proud of having traversed together another of the wild places of our country without the help of a guide.

The next day we rode up Turkey Feather Creek to Turkey Feather Pass. The stream flowed through a narrow, damp gorge which was full of fall flowers of exotic colors. Eventually the gorge gave out and we emerged upon a flat, slightly sloping upland — the Iron Creek Mesa. This was a vast almost level expanse of ponderosa pines, growing wide apart with open savannas between. There was an expansive graciousness in this scene which was new to me — vistas here, there, in every direction along irregular grassy avenues between the trees. One felt the urge to gallop off the trail down these innumerable inviting aisles. Of course the country had been grazed but grazing had now been eliminated in the wilderness area and the grass is coming back in this, the first of the national wildernesses.

Two other special memories I have of the Gila Wilderness. Wednesday afternoon as we were riding up the slope toward the Apache cabin we passed through a stand of aspens, the finest I had ever seen. They were fifteen inches in diameter, tall columns reaching up toward the sun, which shown whitely on their chalk-green bark. Their crowns spread eighty feet above us against a deep blue sky. Looking up those white columns, one lost perspective and reality, and seemed to be moving through a druid temple of which these were the remnant pillars. Never have I seen finer aspens and like some of the weed trees around the Smokies, they furnish one of the most glorious of the seasonal spectacles.

The second memory had also to do with aspens. The next morning we were riding down a slope heading for Mogollon Baldy. Again we passed through a pure stand of aspens. We were high. Fall had already struck. The leaves were a vivid yellow. And the sun shown through them picking up the color until the woods themselves were suffused with a golden haze. It was as though all the riches of the earth had been gathered into that spot and flung broadcast through the air — the golden woods of the Gila.

10

SELWAY-BITTERROOT FOREST
IDAHO
1955

W E HAVE been home five days after another
Wilderness Society Council meeting and field trip in
the west. This time we were chiefly in Idaho, in the
Selway-Bitterroot country. It is an enormous area with a few
primitive roads and little clots of civilization around ranger
stations. We were out for eight days — four days by car and four
by horse. It was beautiful, austere, awesome, and lovely by
turns. We met an extraordinarily fine group of foresters who
were responsible for its care. They were intelligent, dedicated
men with a fine feeling for wilderness.

Lightning fires were their great nemesis and they would use
any measures to confine them — planes, smoke jumpers,
bulldozers. Even though this was a primitive area, fire was an
enemy to be controlled. And there was the stark evidence of the
1934 fire which burned 100,000 acres; and of the 1910 fire,
which burned a larger acreage.

It was difficult for me to understand how, after such extensive fires, any forest would remain at all. The answer seemed to be that all fires were not as devastating as the 1910 and 1934 ones. I am still not completely satisfied. In many of the areas we traversed on our trip, there was abundant forest. Indeed the cedar grove above our camp at Elbow Creek was a truly noble forest. Moreover, the streams seemed clear and lovely with that flat and deceptively placid appearance which is such an engaging characteristic of many western streams.

And so we found roads, back roads, steep and dusty, which gave access to the primitive. One or two spurs seemed unnecessary for fire fighting. Why could they not be abandoned? we asked.

"Oh, the hunters wouldn't let us close them. The packers work out to the road heads to outfit the great elk-hunting parties in the autumn. The crop of elk is nearly fifty percent in excess of the take; the forests are being overbrowsed, so we must give every encouragement to the hunters."

But why, I asked, are there so many elk? This was not great game country in the days of Lewis and Clark. Well, the fires opened up the forests and the elk came in. They crowd out the deer. Elk are very adaptable and can live in areas which do not provide an optimum diet. I wanted to know how such excesses were controlled before the days of the modern hunters with their high-powered rifles and telescopic sights. Here again the answer did not seem sharp to me. But the predators have taken a terrific beating with 1080* stations. Coyotes, cougars, and grizzlies are about gone. There is still a bounty on coyotes and perhaps on the others.

---

*Sodium fluoroacetate.

The primitive area seemed to have become a gigantic elk factory, which was proliferating beyond expectation. The roads had to be kept open to serve the hunters to keep it from getting completely out of hand. The concept of wilderness seemed to be obscured, to say the least. Where was the exquisite balance, or life pyramid about which Leopold had written with such nice understanding and feeling? Had wilderness succumbed to animal nose-counting and fire fighting?

If no fire control were decreed because this was a wilderness, would it open up the forests to forces of destruction which would leave a hot, austere waste for generations to come? If it were decreed that fire should run its course in a designated area, what would be the consequences to man and his preconceptions about wilderness? Would succeeding generations have to live out three or four lifetimes before they could see the forests even in the state we saw them? Did Lewis and Clark see it as we did, or had we run into a dry cycle which was especially hard on the forests?

Somehow I feel we did not get all the answers about this primitive area. How could it have taken such a beating in the one hundred fifty years since Lewis and Clark, who inaugurated there the era of the white man? Were our Forest Service friends rationalizing? I have the highest respect for their professional know-how and integrity, but somehow I would like to know more.

A few days later at the Council meeting at the Murie ranch, Bernie Frank said the Forest Service is fighting twentieth century fires with outmoded techniques. He was of the opinion that fire control research should be pushed — helicopters, fog-sprays, etc. None of these methods would affect the appearance of wilderness and each would open promising avenues for control.

Somehow after the trip through the Selway, I came away with the impression that administrators are sacrificing timeless values to administrative convenience. The question to them is not, "How can I save these values," but "How expeditiously can I do it without too much loss?" Who is to judge what is "too much loss"? The administrators, of course; and so there is a whittling away of remoteness, of the great silences, of the subtle spell of the wilderness.

In the Selway, we found a Forest Service landing field at the very heart of the area and even at our two primitive camps, we were not out of the range of telephones. At Elbow Creek a call was placed for some saddle horses which had gone home to their ranch after a big fight in the night with other horses. And at Indian Lake, a telephone call was made to Missoula. Would the exploits of Lewis and Clark receive such attention if they had had such telephonic aids? And yet in the Selway-Bitterroot forest, where conservationists are trying to preserve a huge area in a wilderness state for future generations, we already find these dilutions.

This brings me to another point about which I commented at the meetings and which I discussed at some length with G. M. Brandborg and Olaus. It is that we as a nation are getting too soft. Thurman Trosper, Forest Supervisor, and others said they can not get men these days to undergo the physical hardships necessary to do these tasks in a simpler way. Ed Hummel, Superintendent of the Great Smokies Park, and El Ogle, a warden, say the same thing in the Smokies.

Olaus feels there is too much emphasis on machinery and horses, and not enough understanding of the adaptability and

toughness of the human body.

Those Forest Service men love the outdoors. Trosper, riding gaily along the trail said,

"Imagine getting paid for this!"

I do not glory in physical exploits for their own sake, but I do stand for rounded experience in which there is a balanced blend of activity – physical, mental, and appreciative. A long walk in gorgeous surroundings tones the body and the appreciations.

Olaus pointed out something else, that dwindling physical strength tends to influence one's thinking and that some, not all, staunch wilderness defenders become diluters as they get older.

Looking ahead perhaps we need to branch out more in *The Living Wilderness.* We need to discuss problems, yes. We also need to discuss appreciations. We need accounts of personal experiences. We need to reflect the awe which many of us felt as we rode and walked for miles through those enormous flats of cedar above Elbow Creek. Those great trees had magnificent proportions. That grove is a prize spot on our continent – little known. Ray Harmon, in charge of Information and Education for Region 1, said he preferred that people come upon it unexpectedly and enjoy it as a part of a total wilderness experience. This viewpoint has both discernment and restraint.

Bernie checked carefully and is of the opinion that the oldest of those trees are about two thousand years – older than the Christian era. What a responsibility to protect them!

Mostly, I think I enjoyed the foliage. At Elbow we washed off "inches" of dust which adhered to us as we came down off the ridge to the creek. I went back to our camp and stretched out on my mattress looking up through the cedars. The flat, light-green, fan-like foliage, through which I looked to the blue of the sky, was lovely beyond words. I lay there for an hour or more trying to engrave forever upon my memory that framework of living beauty above me.

It is interesting, now that I am home, to reconcile my impression of the Selway and Lolo country, which I had obtained from reading, with my impression obtained from actual experience. From my reading I anticipated denser, more varied forests; deeper gorges, more crowded by vegetation. Actually, except in the burns, these are primarily evergreen forests at all elevations. Although there are occasional multiple blowdowns which impede travel, I have yet to observe an evergreen forest in the west which seems as dense and close-packed and inescapable as those in our eastern mountains. Hence even though the slopes were very steep, I had not anticipated the comparative openness of the woods.

Similarly on the Lolo Trail. The dividing ridge was up and down, but there was an openness to it on this August-September date, for which neither the Lewis and Clark *Journals* nor Bob Marshall's writings prepared me. Of course I realize that deep snows, bitter cold, and being afoot could create a vastly different atmosphere.

My impressions of the streams did not require as much reconciliation. They were not overhung, as I expected, and they were not quite as large or forbiddingly wide. The streams at this season seemed to originate in the residual storage of ground waters which were absorbed from the winter season.

I was not disappointed in the Selway nor in the Lochsa rivers. They are magnificent streams, as clear as any Smoky streams, but with a subtle difference I was never quite able to tie down. There was greenness, but it was lighter than the water

91

of streams to which I was accustomed. Perhaps it was because there was more openness and light from the skies. There were even rough stretches of pounding rapids and cascades. But the dominant impression I carried away was of their flat, wide, openness falling gradually, beautifully and clearly mile after mile. These were the salmon-spawning streams, with water-rounded stones as big as your head. There were huge rounded boulders, solid ledges, and shores of flat, water-worn stones, but too fat for skipping stones.

One night at the Fenn Ranger Station, Anne, Doris, and I walked out along the stream and watched it in the moonlight. I loved those deceptively swift streams. The fall was greater than appeared and the rush and swirl of the water around the flat bends and twists of the valleys furnished the living quality of this great wilderness.

11

W E ARE back from ten days in the canoe country of northern Minnesota — three of them actually beyond the pale of motor boats and roads and houses. There were no signs, no radios, no power saws; nothing but hand work, patiently done without too much rush or too much concern for deadlines.

Led by Ernest Oberholtzer, we started out by cabin cruiser northeast across Rainy Lake to one of its utmost arms. At Spawn Inlet we picked up two jolly boatmen and went on about two miles farther to the first portage.

Here we floated the cruiser to the rocky shore — chain-passed packs into a small outboard boat, and then onto land. At the end of the small portage that followed, we packed eleven people plus duffle, into three outboards. One was made of narrow wooden strips and I remember water seeping through a joint in a steady stream. I remarked about it — the others glanced at it casually and were unperturbed. We portaged again very soon to the right of a falls. We were now on Otúkkamamowán, or Trout Lake. For another hour or so we again headed north a dozen or more miles to the limits of Lake Otúkkamamowán. Here we drew into a grassy inlet where we met slim, attractive Jim Banks, an Ojibway Indian, and competent, bouncy Ron Lempi. Everybody helped portage over, including the two boatmen who turned back from there.

Canoes were drawn up on the bank awaiting us. It began to rain and when I made my last trip over, the packs had been covered by a tarp. Some put on slickers, others gathered under the trees, and Jim Banks squatted under a canoe. Ober, in straw cap and a canvas jacket, shivered in the rain and the wind.

It is hard for me to gauge those fellows. They crouched or stood in the rain as casually as though it were a sunny day. Ober, I know, has profound convictions about the place of toil and hardship in attuning one's body. I have heard him tell of not having been dry for weeks at a time on a canoe trip, and of having been wet even a few times at night. Our queries, prior to the trip, about the temperature and the prospects of freezing weather must have seemed trivial to him.

On the other hand, his arrangements for our comfort exceeded anything I have experienced in the wilderness. But there was one great difference. The gear was all transported by arm, back, and leg power. True, we utilized the strengths and skills of those who knew more about the lakes than we. But even so, I don't think we were completely a dead load.

I find myself writing more about the people than I usually do. It was a jolly group. Jim Banks was reserved. He husbanded his words. His face was slim and dark, with flashing black eyes.

There was no flaunting his strength or his competence. He launched the first canoe — packed it, and I joined him as bow paddler. En route he spotted a mink and used one word to call it to my attention, then twisted and turned the canoe until the creature was almost under me — looking up with terror in its eyes before it dived.

I didn't know how far we had to go. I felt awkward, and self-consciously felt I was being weighed in the balances of the north country. Perhaps I was. I asked Jim to criticize my paddling.

"You do all right," he said.

We were going down a narrow inlet. It was late in the afternoon. The banks were not too far away on either side. At length we saw smoke and tents — our first camp. Jim maneuvered around to some shelving rocks. I introduced myself to Ed and Arden Barnes and to Kay Morgan and George Schaller who had preceded us. I felt a little awkward and in the way as we unloaded.

But another storm was coming. Jim said,

"It will rain again." And then I felt at home. How many times have I put up a tent against a rain in the Smokies.

I unrolled our mountain tent, showed Jim how to fit the stakes together and before the others arrived he and I had our tent up. I felt I had gained in his favor and remembered Ober's statement that many of the older Indians have never accepted white people or their ways. Was I, a relatively highly civilized white man, unconsciously seeking the approbation of this silent Indian? I don't know, but I so wanted to feel at home in this new (to me) wilderness country.

The others came into view. Anne was with Ober and was paddling. There was strength and life and appeal in that small

95

flotilla of canoes which came to our landing. I had not reckoned with these brown and gray, infinitely varied rocks of the islands. I had expected steep and precarious landings, but the rocks and their shelvings were abundant and varied. Of course on shore, too, rock was usually close to the surface; that's where we found our air mattresses a comfort.

It rained a little more and a slight fall of hail pointed to violent changes overhead. From an excess of caution, I put a fly over our tent although it was hardly necessary.

We were camped on a point in Crackshot Lake. It commanded a vista to the west and a view to the east. There were heavy woods all about our camp — fir and spruce and poplars and aspens and some maples, besides the ground covering of bunchberry and bearberry. The trees were not large; this area had been logged thirty years before. But the woods were warm and companionable. The islands and points did not look skinned. If there was not richness in the aspect of the woods, neither was there poverty.

But I was seeing only the surface. This Ober made clear. Once in similar country he had seen forty-four moose in a day and two hundred seventy-five in a fortnight. Now in 1956, he said, he might go five weeks and not see one. The reason was not the logging, but the damming of the streams and lakes for the log drives which raised the water levels and drowned out the rice swamps where the moose had thrived. We saw no moose on this trip, nor did we see any bear or deer or other big game. No wonder the old Indians looked with distrust upon the white men. Their world had been destroyed by the white men. Their simple, self-sufficient lives had been blasted.

We saw many evidences of beaver. Twice we saw bald eagles. Once we saw a mink and again a muskrat. We were seldom out of the sound of the bugling of the loons. These things were like bread to starved city people. They must seem like the barest crumbs to those kind and gracious and spirited people who once called this country "home."

One thing seemed unharmed — the water. We drew our water from the lakes — drank it wherever we listed. There was an unceasing stir to it when we were there. Of course there were atmospheric fronts moving in and on. I suppose there are periods of dead calm in the air, but never calm underneath.

Rainy Lake and its connecting rivers and lakes are one watershed. They drain everything north of the Mississippi drainage, and most of that west of Lake Superior and south of the immediate drainage into Hudson Bay. This area has a mean annual precipitation of twenty-four inches a year. The deep gray pile of the reindeer mosses, the velvety green mosses, the woods loam, the huckleberry bushes, the bearberry, gather and hold this rain and snowfall and release it slowly down the streams, down the waterfalls, into the inlets, into the marshes and into the lakes. The calm of the lakes is on the surface. Underneath, their waters are on the move, toward the outlets — toward the greater lakes and rivers below.

And so the water moved on, past our campsite, into the lake, and by a thousand campsites past and present. Currents in the water — currents in the air — whipped freshness and purity and vitality into these vast expanses. In such vastnesses are the seeds of all renewal. Given measureless time, the dams if not replaced will rot and be washed out. The marshes that have been flooded will restore themselves. The moose will reappear on the edges of the lakes, as well as bear and deer and foxes and coyotes and wolves. Perhaps the woodland caribou will drift this far south again. This is what the purifying swirl of water at

97

our campsites meant to me.

The next morning we readied the canoes for a trip up Crackshot, into Whitewater Lake, and perhaps on to Eagle Lake. When he slid his canoe into the lake, Ober said to Jim,

"Who is going with you?"

Jim said, "I take Harvey."

And my heart jumped that those restless, timeless eyes had seen me. I would like to think that some of my pleasure came from a recognition of the oneness of this Indian boy with this environment, emasculated as it was. Perhaps even so, he felt more at ease, more at home here than any city people ever feel under the demands and tugs and stresses of their complex, urban life. He of course brushed white civilization on every hand. He spoke in our tongue. Back on Rainy Lake he operated an outboard motor. He was paid in money. He wore white people's clothing. But this was his country. He was too young to have known it at its best except by the stories of his elders but, wrecked and impoverished as it is, he felt at home. Here, on our trip, was simplicity, the exaltation and resultant weariness of hard work. Here people drew together around the cook fire. Here everyone worked to a common purpose. Indian life had been like that, and he perhaps enjoyed our stumbling and fleeting imitation.

Going up the lake, he always cut corners. He would head close, but always safely out, to every point. He said once in one of the few remarks he volunteered, "I like to paddle close to the shore."

On the shore was enormous detail for those who would look – fractured, broken rocks; twisted strata, contorted intrusions. Here were bird and animal droppings – skeletons which had been sucked clean by scavengers. Here were the trim spruces, the ragged cedars, careless firs, and bunchy pines. Here were the groves of poplar and aspen. Here the multi-colored lichens and mosses; the flush of the blueberry bushes; the flash of the eagles. Here was the detail — the open book — which Jim loved, and which he read with a discernment lost on us.

We passed through a narrow, shallow channel into Whitewater Lake. Great rocks loomed just under the surface. There was a wind behind us and the water was choppy and rough. We turned left to the first portage up Eagle River. This was a simple maneuver since we had only a small pack, the paddles, and my camera. It was the first of a number of portages. Jim carried the canoe over the longer ones. Sometimes when the stream wormed through a narrow crevice in the rocks, we would carry it between us for a few rods without turning it over. The going seemed wilder, more remote. There were more evidences of beavers. Sometimes their dams were thrown across the stream itself. Sometimes we saw fresh mud which they had dropped on the ledges as they were transporting it against their chests from the shore to their dams.

The wind whipped in at us from the west sending phalanxes of wavelets across the water. Once we saw a muskrat, lean and sinewy, swimming in the water. There was an evenness to the skyline. The woods had obviously been logged or burned or both, but there was cleanness and vitality.

Sometimes we canoed through swale, and thin screens of jointed grass. Sometimes we saw heads bobbing in the water and Jim would laugh and say, "water lilies." And always he was right. The bobbing was caused by the wind catching the leaves and throwing them into the air from their customary supine position. Sometimes there were pink blooms; sometimes isolated plants which had floated away from their fellows.

(Ober later commented that broken plants of this sort are an indication that some animal — moose, deer, or muskrat — had been feeding here.)

We mounted another rise over the rocks and saw a wide expanse of water in front of us.

"This is Eagle Lake," said Jim.

A movement caught our eye — a great bird was disturbed and flying to our left. A white rump patch marked it a bald eagle. Jim headed straight across the first stretch of the lake to a bold headland which faced south. There high on the rocks, with dense woods and brush back of us, we were joined by the other canoeists. In alternate sun and shadow under brilliant, streaming, gray-white cloud patterns, we lunched. It was early. But of what consequences were watches here. We had arisen almost with the dawn, had paddled and portaged nearly ten miles. We were hungry and at ease and so we ate. Sometimes Jim sat with us, sometimes he squatted alone looking out over the lake.

We finished lunch to an ominous graying in the west. The wind sharpened and raised little spurting pyramids on the surface of the lake. Jim wanted to fish down below on Whitewater and was glad to leave. He took advantage of every protection from the shore — but when the wind struck us fairly we bent to our paddles and drove across the choppy open stretches. I learned to note the smooth places in the water and found that the wind would die down even before we reached the smoothness.

Then the rain came. I was warm and comfortable. Rain gear would have been awkward. So without a word we drove squarely into the squall. My face was splashed — my sweater and trousers were drenched. It was exhilarating to feel the power in Jim's paddle when I got offbeat. The canoe fairly lunged forward. This was his way. He fought for every gain and then when we came into the lee, he paused and said, "Do you think we should wait for them?" This we did while the shower spent itself. At length we spotted the others struggling around a point into the wind. They had drawn up to the bank during the worst of the squall.

At the last portage before Whitewater, we found the two fishing canoes from our party pulled up on the land. It was grassy there — the sun was burning hot and I lay on my stomach soaking up the sun in an unaccustomed leisure and freedom from care. It seemed I lay there for an hour, hardly conscious of the conversation of the others — enjoying the relaxing warmth of the sun on my back.

The wind died down some. For awhile we paddled leisurely while Jim trolled. He was so sure there would be fish in Whitewater Lake. But after awhile he gave up and we paddled strongly and swiftly toward our camp.

Supper was a hilarious affair around an over-hot campfire. Many there were who were invited to a warm central seat, sheltered by a brush screen from the west wind, who sat it out for a few moments and then dashed to a cooler spot. Even Ober, under the blandishments of the girls, sat down in this warm spot and within two minutes moved away. There was banter and story-telling around the fires.

Once more we slept. The next morning there was a bustle in the air. We were to leave this camp and move on down Crackshot by another arm and back into Trout Lake. Things were packed into knapsacks and cartons. Jim packed an enormous load into his canoe — so huge that the other boys protested, but he said, "It's all right."

He made a place for Anne back of the middle on a soft pack, and soon the three of us were under way. He said he wanted to get off first, because there was not much room at the first portage.

This was a delightful stretch on Crackshot — the water was more placid than it had been the day before, and great, brilliant, white clouds were piled high in the sky. With delight to us and obvious pleasure to him, Jim skirted very close to the shores. The motion of the canoe, measured against the shore was exhilarating; but I always suspected from some deep place in his past, he wanted to float close, to read the signs, to see what had been going on.

At the first portage, he as usual took the canoe — deftly turning it sideways, then bringing it above his head and eventually slipping his hands down the gunwales until the yoke was just back of his neck. Slowly he fitted it to his shoulders and then sturdily moved away. As I looked over the great pile of duffle, he said,

"Leave the heavy packs to me."

Actually I learned to carry a very heavy one — one which he helped me shoulder. And I learned to add our long duffle bag to one of his loads. He seemed to love to balance it across another bag. Anne took the paddles, my camera, and our two knapsacks. We got the load across in two and a half trips.

The second portage was a half mile long and had been freshly cleared by Ron and Jim a couple of days before. The footing was soft, like the forest floor, and we moved slowly and carefully under our heavy loads. We emerged onto a tiny marsh, which barely held our packs and those of the others who caught up with us on this long portage.

Here in the swale we had trouble launching. Jim waded and

shoved and tugged before we became water borne. We paddled
to an especially precipitous and charming island. I got out and
held the canoe while we looked back. Some of the others had
more difficulty than we — and several were launched with only
the stern paddler while the bowman hiked to a point where
there was deeper water and was picked up as they came by.

This was an exposed point where we paused, and it was
bitter and cold as we waited for the others to gather. Jim and
Ober took counsel and we pushed on to an island where they
had hoped to find some late blueberries. I found a vantage high
on the rocks and caught in my camera the whole flotilla of six
canoes moving in toward us.

The third night we camped on an island near a small bay
which looked directly to the north. There we unloaded onto a
shelf and as the last pack was removed from the canoe in which
I was standing it lurched backward and I tumbled into
waist-deep water. I never lost my footing, ending up with one
foot in the water and one in the well-filled canoe. I stepped out,
helped lift it on to the bank and emptied it of water. I then
pitched our tent. Previously we had picked a level spot amongst
some pines near the water — and I stretched our tent there.
There was a slanting ramp of rock down to the water, a great
soft, slippery bed of reindeer moss just to the north. After
changing into dry clothes and rigging a line for my wet ones, I
walked with Doris and Dick over this pad of moss for a view
across the visible stretches of water and across the tiny islets
toward the north. Somehow I felt if I could penetrate the
mystery of what lay before me I would learn the secret of the
North Country.

The water was almost still. There was a cleanness and

quietness and serenity to the scene. The strivings of the day had come to rest. The bluster of rain and wind which we had experienced for two days had ceased. Although there was sharpness in the air, fall had not yet come. Weather and man and season had come to rest together.

There was quietness to the scene, but it was also vibrant. Out of the watery spaces came the musical yodelings of the loons calling out to each other — of depths of water into which they dived as we came too near, of the play of young loons and old loons, of food, of oneness with these great expanses of water. The very wildness of their calls drew a further curtain between me and the mystery I would fathom.

There was a certain lushness to the forest. There was also this chalky, gray moss, like a cushion under our feet, but with a greasy treacherousness if we walked across it rapidly. It belonged here but its hold on those rusty, gray rocks was tenuous. The union of land and vegetation seemed tentative, as on the high peaks of the Smokies. Short seasons, numbing cold, served notice upon all growing things that they were here by sufferance only, and the deepest union of trees and shrubs and moss with the rocky land was never quite achieved. The impression remained that we were far to the north — that even in the softness of the woods, the mother rock was close beneath.

I loved this North Country. I loved the cleanness of the lakes and of the banks. The mere absence of so many things which bid for attention in our normal lives was notable. No winking lights, no signs, no motors, no dust, no litter, no confusion. Just that spreading scene of lake and islands reaching without limit toward the north.

Of course I knew it was not always so peaceful. A week

earlier we had stood on the shores of Rainy Lake as a great south wind tore at its surface. Bands of scudding wavelets flicked across the water with the speed of the wind itself, then whipped back and forth like the cracker on a whip, unpredictable and with awesome speed. Great waves eight feet high had piled upon the far shore.

It was deceptive, this peaceful scene in the lingering twilight. It could be as rough as it was now friendly. It could support quantities of game — as it was now devoid of game. It had supported tribes of people — as it now was nearly bereft of people.

Damage had been done. It was not as wild as it had been. But the conditions of recovery were here. There was little or no erosion. There was no lowering of the water table. A young forest was everywhere, ready to grow to maturity. Game would come back, given the chance.

Primitive people might not come back. Their world had become more complex. The wild world might be less complex, more simple. But people seldom retreat to a more simple world. Races almost never. Even if the dams rotted out, even if the level of the lakes dropped to their historic marks, people would not come back to live.

Animals with their simple urges never lose the capacity to live in wilder country. Return for them is simply the renewal of the ancient urges and instincts. Given reasonable protection, they would move back into this environment as natural water levels and returning vegetation favored their needs. But for man, movement is seldom toward the simpler environment.

After our meal of soup from Pennsylvania, of corn from Minnesota, of peaches from California, and of other things from here and there, packaged and made portable to this far place, a supper which contained not one item drawn from the environment, not even a fish, I walked back to that rocky point alone. I stood and then sat for an hour or more looking out to the north. I did not, could not, encompass this country. I had never lived there — never gone through a season. I was simply viewing it within the span of a four day trip. If it were beautiful and serene, I might carry back the impression it was always beautiful and serene. It had not been. There had been a variety of weather — wind and squalls, clouds and even hail. And there was a nudge of fall in the air as I sat on that rock which still retained some of the warmth of the day.

I looked long and felt that I was an outsider. The world was at peace for the moment. The placid water reflected long streamers of light from the planets. There was no moon, but the boundaries of land and water were visible. There were a few insect sounds and occasional stirrings among the loons. Out there in that vastness which was their home even at night, like watchmen along the coast, the loons in a flurry of loon conversation brought themselves up to date on what was going on. No wonder it seemed too inscrutable to me as I tried to make sense, to find a pattern in this limited, fragmentary experience.

12

CLOUD PEAKS
WYOMING
1957

T HE PREPARATIONS necessary for a large pack trip have
been obscure to me — perhaps accepted without
particular thought. This year, because we stayed on at the ranch
a couple of days after the trip was over, we saw some of the
enormous effort involved. At the height of our trip into the
Cloud Peak Primitive Area there were twenty-eight horses, and
counting the stock of the two Forest Service men who were
with us, there were thirty in all. Doctor Will Schunk had fifteen
horses of his own. This meant that he had to get thirteen from
other sources. They brought with them personalities as different
as those of people.

Mine was an enormous black horse who was so tall I could
hardly reach his stirrups. Toward people he was gentle and
tolerant. When I was taking pictures he would stand
contentedly without hitching, chewing at such grass as was

available. But toward his fellow horses, he was a demon. He would bite and lunge and down in Medicine Park, started a stampede in the rope corral as we were trying to get the horses haltered after grazing. I called him "Napoleon." He was an import from another ranch, and was unquestionably the best known horse in the string before the trip was over.

Each horse was different. One young horse in the string had never been packed before. He would bite and kick when they tried to put a pack on him. Chuck McGlothlin, our chief packer, said this was partly because everybody was a stranger to him. He would shy at the canvas tarp and once Chuck rubbed the tarp back and forth under his neck until he realized that it would not hurt him.

Packing seemed to take endless time but on those rough, narrow trails, packs could easily become unbalanced, would slip on the horse, and would have to be straightened or repacked. On our hardest day, the seventh, the pack of that skittish young bay slipped completely around until it was hanging underneath his belly. The contents of the panniers were a mess and there were some exciting moments as they unpacked and adjusted his harness.

Packing was an art which took lots of time and paid off in an uneventful day. Each pannier or duffle was carefully hefted and placed so there would be no unbalance.

This is but background for the brave array of thirty horses and twenty-three people which moved out on the first day for Lake Geneva. We followed an old road for some miles, a road which was so rough we could see spots where folks had punctured their oil pans on protruding rocks, draining the oil into the road. We passed several camps with tents and horses —

108

fishing parties.

In the late afternoon, I found myself alone by a beautiful lake. I could see a meadow at the upper end, and a tent. This was Lake Geneva — "the second most beautiful lake in the Big Horn Mountains." It was rock girt, but had a fringe of trees and opened out to the north. A waterfall pounded down from the southwest. The meadow was extensive, was laced by several streams, and was interspersed with clumps of spruces.

We hunted a place to sleep. One place proved to be mosquitoey. We moved nearer the camp and laid out our beds under a huge spruce which was more than three feet in diameter.

There was one wall tent. The two foresters had another — a teepee. Although we had a dry night, it began to rain in the early morning and we packed our duffle and carried it into the big tent. On the evening before, we had had a lot of jollity and some singing around a big campfire. Zahnie kept things lively with his "speech" about the French republicans and his giving the "pitch" for the songs. Just when things were languishing Woody Williamson, one of the foresters, picked up a song with the clearest tenor I ever heard. It was as though the beauty and sweetness of all the Big Horns had been distilled into that one voice.

The rain came on fast the next morning. The fellows rigged a tarp over the cooking operations where Louise Francis (Dr. Schunk's daughter) and Virginia Demchok presided. Then those that were eating needed shelter and further tarps were rigged up in a Goldbergian conglomeration of makeshift ropes and drains. Water collected in the tarps and had to be drained periodically. The fireplace was in a low spot and the water would not drain away. All ditches were directed to a deep sump which someone dug. Every now and then one of us would take a bucket and empty the sump. Whole trees were carried in and put on a roaring campfire a few feet from the cooking fire. Boots, socks, and clothing were dried and scorched. Hardly a cowboy had a whole shoe sole left after those drying operations!

The poor horses stood out in the rain, tethered to trees, and shivered over their entire bodies. The packers were worried and would go out and pet them and move them under larger trees and closer together where they could get warmth from each other. About noon when the rain was hardest, Chuck and Doctor Will gave each of the horses a ration of oats.

Clouds obscured the mountains about us and as the day grew colder, mists rose off the surface of the lake and obscured the far end. During a particularly bitter fall of rain we noticed whiteness amongst the raindrops. It was sleet, which collected in windrows around the tent.

A hard decision had to be made. If we stayed in camp, we fell one day behind on a tight schedule. But it was next to impossible to pack and move in that wintry rain. So the weather forced our hand and we carried in wood, rigged more tarps, dug more ditches, and made occasional forays out into the weather.

After lunch the rain seemed to lighten a bit and Brandy suggested walking up the trail to see if we could see wild sheep. We plodded slowly up steep switchbacks which were soft with mud. Gaunt trees loomed out of the mists. Some which had died in a forest fire had been burnished by years of sun and weather into a rich copper color. At length we topped the first switchback and Roger Marshall and I walked on to see if we were near the top. Actually we were far from the top. We passed a little lake on our right and then came to a beautiful upland meadow. At the upper end the trees gave out and as the clouds lifted momentarily we looked up to a bare rocky gunsight of a pass. It did not seem too far distant and we decided to push on. All trees disappeared. Grass and turf appeared among the rocks, and there were bare ledges to right and left. We saw the caved-in remains of an old mine and soon we were in the windswept chill of the pass.

On the return we met the others on the benches above the meadow — Anne, George, Brandy, Doris.

As we descended farther there were breaks in the fog. We saw high mountains and snow fields all about us, and at the head of the switchbacks, we looked through a hole in the fog down upon Lake Geneva. The storm was breaking. At the camp the others disbelieved our story that we had climbed to the pass *on foot;* but when we described it, they had to concede that we had been there.

After supper, we retired early and lay under the big tree under our nylon tarp and talked with the Leonards luxuriously into the night.

Friday dawned clear. All tarps came down and things were sunned. There was the bustle of packing, and at last we got under way. I followed Louise, who was leading. On the switchbacks a pack slipped and I took her lead horse while she went back to help. I rode on to the top of the switchbacks for a marvelous view of the lake. Anne said I made a brave silhouette against the sun with my two horses.

Eventually others came up, and on this second trip to the pass in two days, it seemed that we reached it in a very short time. Of course we were riding, but the skies were open and we could see ahead and see the mountains around us. At the gap my own pack slipped and the young horse went to his knees.

111

But others were there to help and they got him to his feet without mishap. Napoleon distinguished himself by stepping on a rein and breaking it.

Over the pass we saw two lakes and hundreds of domestic sheep. These sheep were there legally under old permits, but they were too numerous and had eaten the range down to mineral soil. Broad-leaved weeds were coming in and there were bare, granular areas with no soil whatever. We were above timber line and these milling, baaing sheep were competing for the scant forage with deer and elk and wild sheep.

There was a certain freedom to riding above timber line. The air was light and invigorating. We could see infinite distances. The vegetation was simple and comprehensible. Life was limited; the growing season short. Here was simplicity. Thoreau would have loved it. On a rocky eminence above the trail, Louise found an arrowhead. This had been Indian country.

Eventually we clambered up a sharp rise and then, almost so close we could touch it, there appeared above us the black serrations of Blacktooth Mountain. Zahnie had hung back to hear our exclamations at the sight. Then down to a milky green lake with a tumbling waterfall pouring out of a great snowy cirque. We found a few clumps of timber line trees to shade us from a merciless sun. Nearly everybody had a headache – from the sun and altitude. There we ate lunch and then divided into two parties. Anne because of her headache joined the pack horses for a swift ride to Cliff Lake.

The rest of us followed a precipitous switchback to a shoulder of Blacktooth. We were very high. It was cold and windy and I tied my handkerchief over my beaten hat to hold it on. We clattered over a rocky ridge and then up a high, boggy meadow for a view to the east into Highland Park and Kearney

Lake, where we expected to be three days later.

Leaving my horse with Louise I ran back on foot to a boggy place which was broken with tussocks of grass. I threaded my way through this and sank deeply into mud before I reached firm ground above a clump of cottony, windblown flowers – the cotton flower. This bed, ten or fifteen feet square, was fragilely beautiful – perhaps the most beautiful thing I saw on the trip.

From this meadow Doc led us up a further rocky slope along an intricate pathway which dodged most of the ledges to a tiny plateau-like meadow which looked across a deep glacial gulch to Blacktooth itself. It would have been possible, I suppose, to have followed ridge and snowbank around the head of the cirque to Blacktooth. But we were content to photograph it from our high grassy vantage point. We were close to twelve thousand feet high. Later we learned it is impossible to get to the top of Cloud Peak with horses, because of the rocks. As I look back on it, it was quite a feat for Doctor Schunk to find a connected way through the great talus slopes to this high eminence.

We returned to the lake where we had lunched. It was only as we descended that I became aware of the steepness of the slopes we had ascended. This was no ordinary dude trip. Doc knew his mountains. He knew what was possible, and with mastery and nonchalance he carried us to the limits, it seemed, of what was possible on a horse. The horses stood almost on their heads as they jolted down those slopes. Eventually a catch in my knee caused me to dismount and I led old Napoleon down to the gentle benches above the lake. When I looked back the rest of them seemed to be crawling down a vertical face.

I can't recall much of the ride to Cliff Lake. There we found a level place and laid out our beds, and as the sun cast horizontal rays over the campsite, some of us went swimming. The water was cold, as were the evening breezes, and I quickly chilled.

As we ate, a murkiness came into the western sky and lightning flashed in the north. As others began to fear rain, I noticed a band of light come under the clouds to the west. I was very tired, and was happy we would be able to sleep out, and not have to crowd into that tiny tent. As the skies brightened later, some of us watched the greenish pendant of a comet.

This was the Cliff Lake campsite. We were camped on high ground at the lower end of the lake where a clear stream brawled between us and the vertical face of a mountain just opposite us. It seemed climbable along some angular ledges but no one tried it. The next day we followed this noisy stream down through indifferent country to Teepee Pole Flats. In the valley we found Herefords grazing, and the willows along the stream were stripped and mangled. The cattle had made little terraces along the banks — a sound example of overgrazing.

After lunch we left the valley of North Paint Rock Creek, as a storm gathered in the west and we climbed steep forested slopes to the south. At one point, because of the danger of lightning, Louise halted the party just before we would cross an exposed ridge. Later we moved on through sleet and wind, down into a beautiful upland meadow with a lilied lake and more cattle. After awhile we descended rather steeply through lodgepoles to a tiny meadow through which flowed the main Paint Rock Creek which drained Lake Solitude.

Again my mind is almost a blank. I recall that we rode upstream to an opening among lodgepole pines, where we got our first glimpse of Lake Solitude. It was a jewel of a lake, far

114

from civilization, with enormous gray cliffs on either side and a low meadow at the upper end — our destination. The trail was first through lodgepoles and then through a talus slope of gigantic rocks — some as big as a house. In this tumbled nightmare, a way had been blasted by dynamite and built up by hand, the crevices being filled in with glacial sand. In this terrifying area, where a misstep by our mounts could mean a fall and a broken leg, Louise suggested that for safety's sake we ride with our feet out of the stirrups. The old trail we were told, had followed high on the cliffs above the worst of the talus slope. If this were better, we could imagine what the old trail was like!

I wish I could write more about Lake Solitude. It is perfection among lakes. In the ups and downs of our trip we had reached a new climax. Chuck told us that the surveyor who first came into this country did not give a name to a single lake until he came to this one. He named it "Solitude."

The boys had previously pitched a big canvas tent, and several teepee tents over the meadow. It was broken by three streams which poured in from the heights to the east. Low willows lined these streams, and clumps of spruces grew near the lake. Lodgepoles clung in hedges to the south cliffs and a solid forest grew down into the southeast corner of the flats. A long grassy bench overlooked the meadow on the north. And there among spruces and grass-covered rounded ledges, Anne and I found a sheltered hollow for our bed. We were now above eight thousand feet, and I puffed as I carried our duffle up to the grassy bench.

Bernie fished from the edge of the lake and I watched a rainbow-colored sunset as clouds formed in the west. We built up a campfire, the flames of which whirled like an egg beater

115

before the erratic winds.

We retired early to our open beds. The stars were myriad in number and of unparalleled brightness. From our bench we looked up into them as from the top of the world. And then we slept.

I awoke with a start. The long rays of the sun were poking luminous magic through the ranks of the lodgepoles opposite us. It was past seven o'clock. I said,

"I have to get up," and I fumbled for my camera and fumbled into my clothes and boots. Never have I slept so soundly and seldom have I ever awakened more slowly. My mind was alert, however, and I drove my unwilling body up through the aspens and spruces and the ledges above us to vantage points from which to photograph the lake. It was brilliant and a glory in the morning sun.

This day which began so propitiously was to heap climax upon climax. As we ate breakfast, ominous arching clouds hung over the heights to the east, the direction in which we were to go. We saddled up the horses, leaving the pack horses behind and started up the trail.

A waterfall pounded out of a hollow to the left. The Schunks are not ones to keep to the beaten trail. Soon they left the Forest Service trail and took to the north slopes. There was no trail. It was simply a route over which they had been, but not for eight years. Sometimes we were on a game trail; sometimes searching out the way along parallel shelves of rock. Twice we had commanding views back to Solitude, the second time near timber line. Leaving this we moved god-like in magnificent open country of grassy ledges and reefs of rock. The grass became long and luxuriant. We were beyond all grazing. We were in the short season between winter — and

116

winter in an area of such violent weather and cliffs that only wilderness people like the Schunks ever came here. Somehow they imbued their horses with the will to go and somehow we outlanders never feared to go over slopes which had seemed only for movies and cowboys.

Once we were held up for long minutes as those in the lead opened a way down through a thick copse, so steep that we had to lead our horses. I was terrified that old Napoleon might slip and fall on me. But he, like all the others, proved to be sure-footed and we descended one hundred twenty-five vertical feet without mishap. On and on through this fantastic back country, looking down upon remote lakes, upon hundreds of isolated boulders left thousands of years ago by the receding glaciers like checkers on the bare rocky bones of the mountain.

Finally, we descended to a tiny meadow hemmed in by cliffs, by a lake, and by a slithering, almost horizontal cascade which drained over bare rock. This lake, above timber line and known only to the Schunks and their friends, to which they had found a way by incredible perseverance, was the wildest, remotest place I had ever been. The willows along the stream were mere shrubs. Grass was long and luxuriant. It was the first time I was to see what a wild range could be like. Flowers were sparse but beautiful. The Schunks by herculean endeavor had stocked this lake with fish, but Bernie was unable to raise one. Doctor Will called it Fish Lake. Nobody but the Schunks ever went there.

George Marshall and I splashed through the cascade and moved out on the rocky benches to the north. Going was easy on the bare rock and we came down to the stream which connected with another lake. Here we saw pipits and water ouzels. We decided to follow the grassy fringe around the lake,

117

and as we came opposite the ledges, we saw that others were following. They called to us to return, saying that they wanted to walk to the next lake. We returned, teetering on hummocks of grass and splashing through gleaming rivulets seeping down from the snow fields.

And so we proceeded along the edge of the upper lake, now through grass, now around a ledge, now through frightful blocks of talus. We hoped to see elk, but as we rounded ledge after ledge we were always disappointed. However, the remoteness was as enspiriting as a view of elk. There was no evidence of man. Long grass whipped in the wind. Flowers grew undisturbed. The grass grew scarcer; rocks and talus, more predominant. I outdistanced the others, climbed a little slope, and looked into a giant cirque at the very foot of Cloud Peak. It was gray and forbidding and austere. Only the barest tinge of green touched the rocky shelves.

I had reached the foot of another slender lake and at its upper end a great cascade as noisy as New England surf boomed over bare rock. Above it was a basin which tapped snow fields high on the south slope of Blacktooth.

The roar of those waterfalls seemed incongruous in those rocky surroundings so far from the seashore. The booming had the quality of heavy surf — with one difference. This sound was continuous whereas the sound of surf is intermittent. The falls flow steadily although there was sone re-echoing in those high cirques, but the surf gathers itself in surges as the waves roll in. The incessant thundering of the cascades was stirring and in character with the violent and implacable cliffs which they drained.

Will said he doubted if two dozen people had ever been to that spot. We rested and luxuriated in that colossal scene. The roar of the great cascade, which Chuck said was fed by a chain of seven lakes, filled the air. Here was the raw creation of mountains untouched and ungrazed, where man might visit but where he could never live. This was the farthest I had ever been from civilization. Even those sure-footed horses, two lakes down, could not reach here. We were at the very apex of man's penetration of this violent area. We left reluctantly. I don't know just why. There are things about the wilderness, which we who support and defend it, do not understand. We only know that we deeply love it and that it is as deeply satisfying.

On the return to the horses we saw where the stream snuggled closely against a straight-sided ledge. Chuck called it a mill race. We saw an igneous dike which stretched from stream to mountain top. It had fallen out cleanly like a loose filling from one's tooth, and had tumbled into a huge pile. The rock was dark brown and muddy-colored where we crossed it. Dikes were everywhere in this land – in whirls and twists and in ranks which marched straight across the country.

As we neared the horses we heard a shout and saw Zahnie silhouetted far above us on bare rock, where he had climbed barefooted.

Napoleon, true to his big-footed clumsiness, had stepped on and broken another rein, which George found after a search of the little valley. Zahnie crushed the luncheon cans and we brought them all out, leaving no trace of our visit.

We made quick time on the return. At the steep place we went up three at a time, resting twice on the ascent. Bernie was in the second group. Louise and Virginia had tied their horses and had come back to watch the others. As Bernie came by his horse hesitated and looked at the girls. It was no place to stop and Bernie, apprehensive, said to his horse,

119

"Never mind the women; get on up to that level place."

When it came Anne's turn to go up, she was nervous and wondered whether her horse could make it. Just as she started, Zahnie called to her:

"Anne, what does this remind you of in the Smokies?"

Concentrating on the climb, she was upset by the interruption, and answered rather sharply, "Nothing." Zahnie chuckled and said, "That's right."

Chuck came up last on that magnificent little horse of his and she trotted nearly all the way.

On the sixth day we started out the same trail as on the fifth day, but kept on up the Forest Service trail. We looked across the valley and saw the route to Cloud Peak. No horse could climb that pile of rock. We saw meandering streams in a meadow. We saw a deer ensconced in an open place in the woods across from us. Louise came back for us. She liked to keep the group closed up.

"Things happen when you get strung out," she said.

She pointed out Bomber Peak where a plane crashed during the war. We circled the lake of the Misty Moon at timber line. Bernie and I discussed the grouping of trees at timber line. He thought the hoop of limbs around the base of the trees was a self-protective adaptation to the rigor of the environment.

We came to an enormous peak with a vertical side and dark streaks of water seeping down. Two lakes clung to its base and a third caught the water from them. This was Golden Lake. Here was a fine meadow with great round tussocks of grass. Here we ate with a rocky knoll back of us, that huge cliff in our face and shallow Golden Lake below us. The pack horses filed across the sward above Golden Lake – a moving sight.

I climbed the talus to the foot of the vertical cliff for

120

pictures, then returned to my horse and moved on with Anne and Louise to Florence Pass.

The high point of the pass was under Bomber Peak. We found a cornice of snow and a lake; there was little vegetation. It was a high, cold, grim place. We followed the shore of the lake and looked down a monstrous V made up of waves of rock which had rumbled from the peaks above. It was forbidding, a merciless spot — subject to rock fall — and the trail had been realigned and filled in artificially with gravel through some of the worst places. In several spots flows of the rock falls had met above the true bottom of the valley erasing the stream. Somewhere deep in the interstices it found its way to burst forth below, cleanly and sweetly.

After long hours, the trail and stream debouched into a long, grassy valley with some trees. This was Medicine Park where we camped. But beetling cliffs rose across from us and broad potato-shaped cliffs mounted back of us. There were numerous snow fields not a thousand feet above us. I was fascinated and wanted to climb to the nearest snow field. But the scree below it was so steep and loose, I settled for the talus slope of huge rock chunks just opposite our grassy camp. The talus stones were sharp and easily climbed but were in precarious balance, and several of them grumbled hollowly as I passed over them. One slipped under foot and crashed sickeningly as I stepped forward. I soon came to the cliff face itself where there was a thin line of vegetation. This gave reasonably firm footing and I moved rapidly upward.

I could see the others, very tiny, down in the valley watching me. Apparently, against the cliff I was not always visible. Several times I took to the cliff but was forced back by loose rock. Although a part of the cliff, these loose chunks were laid up insecurely as in a dry wall. I did not dare risk clambering over them and did not want to move around them alone. Anne said Doctor Will watched me uneasily and wanted to know how old I was. At length I came down, picking up samples of vari-colored rock on the descent.

After supper we had comic relief when Louise and Virginia marched Jim Francis into the meadow in an effort to force him to wash and change into fresh clothes. He broke away from them and ran leaping across the meadow toward the cliff with the two in pursuit. When they closed in on him he took to the talus and ran up it like a mountain sheep. As they followed below him, I was afraid that he would set loose a stone upon them. Finally, as a compromise, Louise carried his clothes over to a great rock as he shouted to Virginia to go back. He changed behind the rock while the girls waited.

After supper clouds gathered in the yosemite to the west of us. As dark came, rain seemed certain. Anne and I went to our little bench just above the valley floor and had just gotten to bed when the rain came. It rattled on our tarp but we had too much of it beneath us and our heads got wet. After the first rain, I got out in my bare feet and pulled more of the tarp from beneath us and over us. Our duffle we rested on one poncho, pulling the flap over and spreading the second poncho on top. This sufficed.

The next rain was a battering thunderstorm of nearly three-fourths of an inch. The rain came down in huge drops which bombarded our bodies as we snuggled under the tarp. The very ground seemed to shake beneath us. But we did not get wet except for condensation. However, our endurance was tested as we lay so long without moving or stretching because of the storm. One hand went to sleep and I had to fight against a feeling of suffocation.

After that storm we threw the covers back for awhile until a third shower came, about daylight. When we looked out at last, the skies were clearing and the snowline had crept a thousand feet down the mountain.

Morale was low that morning and there was talk of riding on into Sheridan. But as the sun came out, we reset our course to the original objective, Highland Park, even though spectacular clouds boiled about.

Clear Creek flowed down between three parallel sets of moraines. What a straight course the glaciers had held after they burst from the confines of the valley. All of the moraines were forested and as we looked back on them from the far slope they lay before us like a diagram.

Again we climbed to timber line where we met a boy with two pack horses carrying supplies to sheep herders.

At Frying Pan Lake we had a sleet storm and we huddled amongst some giant spruces for lunch. On and on, down through Willow Park and over a low divide into Kearney Creek. As we crossed this Bernie and I noticed that it had been gouged deep as by a huge flood. He thought it might have been from placer mining but Will said it had been from a break in Kearney Dam thirty years previously.

It was getting late. We were moving through a thick forest of lodgepole. The riders were strung out. We came to a plunging jam of horses. The bay's pack had slipped and was hanging from its belly. Dwayne dashed off for Chuck. Doc and Roger stopped to help. I went on alone with Dwayne's lead horse. I came to Kearney Lake and a maze of trails. As I was wandering around Roger came on alone. Louise came charging back to set us aright. We went up steeply through deepening darkness. I could hardly see the trail. We came to a jam of horses again. The others, confused and uncertain, had stopped. We had been in the saddle ten hours, and had covered twenty-five miles. Chuck and Doc rode ahead and came back to report we were within five minutes of a campground. We rode on. The air was sharp, the sky crisp. I said it would be clear and cold that night. Doc added, "Damn cold."

We had a great fire and heated soup and chili. I helped Chuck and Doc with the horses. We went to bed and slept.

I was up at 5:30 and helped Will make an Indian fire. I chopped an old snag for very dry wood. There was frost on the packs. The creek where we washed and got our water was numbingly cold. Doc pointed out a snow field a few hundred yards away from which it flowed.

We were again just at timber line and after starting on, burst into the clear a couple of hundred yards above the camp. We came to a great rolling pass. Below us was the huge meadow of Highland Park. Beyond and higher were the jagged outlines of Blacktooth and the rounded summit of Cloud Peak.

The pack horses went on. The rest of us rode to the edge of the canyon for photos. Now thoroughly at home with Napoleon, I rode all over the park and would drop the reins when I stopped. He would stand and eat while I photographed. We crossed another pass going north and missed a turn and went deep down the East Fork of Little Goose River before discovering our error. It was rough with nasty switchbacks. We plodded wearily back and found the trail marked by cairns through a boulder field. Anne and I stopped for pictures, and as we reached the next pass we met Louise who had trotted back looking for us. We were again above timber line on a high slope overlooking Cross Creek and Big Goose.

The views were stupendous. We could see the cirque of Lake Geneva and the domed rock back of the Schunk cabin and the long forested ridge separating Cross Creek and Big Goose. Clouds threatened. There was a mild sleet storm. We pushed on. The horses picked up speed, and Napoleon won a mad race. After we passed the gate he ran again. He galloped madly into the lead and held it into Jackson's ranch, whence we had started our trip eight days before.

There we unpacked. The pack horses were turned loose and dashed off with Chuck. The rest of us followed on horses five more miles to the Schunk cabin, which we reached in late afternoon. After unsaddling, there was a flash of lightning and a hail storm with stones as big as marbles. They rested an inch thick on the ground. What would our horses have done in that storm? As it was, they burst madly from the paddock for the shelter of the trees.

Before supper we took a Finn bath and our travels were over.

13

THIS YEAR members of the Wilderness Society Council had two field trips. One was along the Washington coast from Cape Alava south to La Push. The protection of this strip of almost unmarred coast has been a consuming interest of Justice William O. Douglas. He wanted a small group of three or four hikers. But as on the Chesapeake and Ohio Canal trip, the small group mushroomed into a party of seventy people.

We were driven over to the north end of Ozette Lake in three buses. We went by back roads of the Rayonnier Corporation. Along the road there was some magnificent timber. There were many patch cuttings and some burned country. There were raw, bulldozed roads, and a general air of neglect which is often found where money is the prime desideratum. Man is dependent upon the earth covering for his very existence. This forest was raw dollars-and-cents stuff which

126

is transmuted in the maw of industry into cash in banks, and into stocks and bonds. Of course it goes into houses and paneling and paper and newsprint. But civilization — that curious stockade of the spirit with which mankind surrounds itself — so often gives the forest a value only as it relates to its culture and to industry, and ignores it as a place for study, for inspiration, and as a pointer to the ultimate meaning of life.

We emerged upon the east shore of Ozette Lake, proceeded from the north end of the lake up an old road, and then turned into the woods on a trail which was heavily corduroyed. The trail was perfectly dry. The woods seemed dry. The ravines, which crossed our path and were tilted toward the Ozette River, had little or no water.

The end of the lake was less than one hundred feet above sea level but we climbed some, through magnificent rain forest, and emerged onto a broad plain which stretched widely in all directions. The trail was flanked with deep blue gentians.

We entered the forest again, climbed a little and then crossed a flat summit after which we began to hear the low roar of the ocean. We descended on a slant through an understory of shoulder-high ferns. Through a screen of trees we could see water. There were no marshes; there was no transition. We stepped from dense forest onto massive driftwood and thence onto the beach. This was Cape Alava.

Unspoiled coast stretched some thirty or forty miles north, and about twenty-five miles to the south. There had been a little mining, and an Indian village or two (we saw some shell mounds). But where the forest remained uncut and where no roads penetrated, ocean and forest had a way of healing themselves and it seemed to me that the area must have been as little marked as when Balboa himself first looked out upon the

Pacific thousands of miles to the south.

John Osseward remarked that there was one difference which my untutored eye had not detected. For miles we found a buffer of driftwood between the beach and the forest. It was made up of huge saw logs from eighteen inches to eight feet in diameter. They had been tossed up in a massive jumble as far inland as the waves could hurl them. The old ones were weathered a chalky white. The new ones were a battered brown. They were all saw logs which had broken away from rafts to drift and be thrown willy-nilly onto the beaches. Thirty years ago, John told me, the belt of driftwood was composed of whole trees with wildly branching root systems as high as a house. That period antedated the logging days. Great trees would be undercut by floods and thrown into the streams. They would then float out to sea and ultimately be cast high on the beaches in a storm.

As a rule the drift logs paralleled the shore and, where the sand or pebbles were loose, we sometimes walked along them for considerable distances, stepping from one log to another. But at times also we would come to the end of a great butt and would be forced to jump six or eight feet to the beach.

At our first camp near Sand Point the cordon of logs was both high and deep and we had to cross it to reach fresh water. Here some prior adventurers had laid a precarious pathway of planks from log to log. Tricky as it was, it was simpler than plunging from log to log. I tried this once, and a great log rolled under my weight.

The dry weather had lowered the streams. At Sand Point we drank from a pool of water back in the forest. It was fresh but did not flow.

We scraped smooth a place amongst the driftwood and slept

on the sand. It was a prodigal experience. In addition to the logs there were planks and boards and pieces of boxes, twigs, and branches. An ax was hardly needed. Wood, slightly water logged but burnable, was everywhere and in prodigious quantitites.

This was a nice, firm, wide sandy beach between the drift belt and the water. Even at high tide the waves filming out to nothingness on the gently shelving beach did not reach the drift. I could only speculate, with nothing but my imagination to go on, as to the pounding fury of the storms which would fling those colossal logs onto the shore. People could not hurt the beach by mere camping — the first storm would obliterate all signs. The ocean here is self-cleansing, and, if left alone, is self-healing.

I was struck by the fact that everyone on the trip was drawn to the water. They would stride purposefully toward the waves as though they were going to walk all the way to Japan. And then a higher wave would send them scrambling back. I rolled my pants and waded in the semi-frigid (54°) water. It had a soothing and healing effect upon my tired feet. Some would stand and look, silhouetted against the cascading waves. Some, including Bill Douglas, strolled the beach. Some went bathing — some washed pots and pans — some took pictures. The parade was constant — the purposes, as diverse as the people themselves. But the ocean, with its restless movement, its surging, breaking waves, its constant slapping roar and immeasurable vistas dominated us. Sometimes its force was muted by fog, and the knob-like islands grew gray and distant or disappeared entirely. But as we walked and slept I had no feeling that we were on the beach *between* the ocean and the forest, or that we were on the edge of the forest. The power and presence of the ocean was so overpowering, it was completely dominating. The sea was, indeed, around us.

That night the ocean was dimmed by fog. Sometimes we could see a ghostly ship far to the north – sometimes it vanished in the haze. But the timeless booming of the sea was unstilled. As we slept, the tide crept up toward us and receded. Once I awoke. The fog had vanished and in the moonlight the water stretched endlessly. On the horizon I could see something like a light grow into incandescence and then streak to the right and left. What mystery was this? Was there an aurora of the sea? I wanted to call out and ask. But all were sleeping peacefully and quietly. And then it came to me – it was the rollers far out, breaking into white and incandescence under the glow of the moon. The streaming light was the white water following the crest of a roller which had started to break.

I was a novice. The sounds and sights and brackish odors, the omnipresent sand sifting into our boots and clothes, the disarray of the drift, the bleached and whitened logs, the rolling sound, the rolling water contributed to an experience I found to be overwhelming.

Sig Olson has written that at a Listening Point on one of the northern lakes, he began to clutch at the meaning of life. Here, I was grasping at meanings which were as elusive as the fog itself. Meaning to me was an amalgam of quiet ecstasy, boundless curiosity, serenity, appropriateness, and humility. This did not have to be valued or equated or understood, ever. It was there to be absorbed through every nerve in my body – without jarring intrusions. I think that is what this beach is for – in man's little world. And so I slept and drowsed and felt and thought – on this strip of Pacific coast.

The next morning there was fog. The Justice said it was a typical summer day along the coast. We started early – 6:30, as

I recall. We weren't going to work. We punched no time clocks. It was the tide which governed our movements. If we reached those points of rock at the proper time we could work our way around them. If not, we had to wait, or climb a saddle of loose soil and rock, covered with fragile vegetation. I climbed one about one hundred feet high and worked around the end of another and across a swag of disintegrating rock. The waves were not too bad. They could be timed and avoided. The rock was firm and sharp. But this neck was steep and covered with loose stones above a trough of hard rock. I made it with the help of Brandy and Donald Murie. And then the shore opened out onto a serene beach.

Sometimes we worked across flats of cobblestones, greasy with seaweed. The cobbles were of every size. We tried to avoid the seaweed. Where this could not be, we tried to wedge our feet in between the stones. Everybody had his own private formula. One avoided anything that was brown in color – rock or seaweed. I did not follow the brown formula, but avoided if I could anything which was wet, except sand or the logs. Some of the rounded cobbles gave excellent footing when dry. Much of the rock seemed to be a kind of limestone which weathered sharply.

Douglas moved with the tides. He rose early and moved fast. There was comment by the photographers that he hiked very rapidly.

The second day we encamped just beyond a steep point still connected with the mainland. Some called it Allen's Point. It was about two hundred feet high. A Coast Guard lookout had surmounted it during the war. No name appeared on the map. But being high over the ocean, and still connected with the land, it supplied sweeping views up and down the coast. We worked around it at low tide.

We camped about two p.m. The woods were close, beyond a little ridge of gravel and the usual array of driftwood. We followed a zigzagging bridge of gigantic logs and laid our beds under a great fir tree on a mat of dead bracken. It was a glorious, sheltered place, about which someone said,

"This looks like the place where Adam gave birth to Eve."

Anne and I were traveling light — using no mattresses — and those dead ferns provided a dry and fragrant bed. Again we drank from pooled water.

The view from the Coast Guard hut was commanding. The rock fell away so steeply, its base was not visible. Much of the day's route and most of the camping area could be seen. The sunset was simple — nothing but sun and sea. Not an island, not a tree. But from sun and sea have come nearly everything we know. How simple the view; how profound the meaning.

Above I commented that we were completely dominated by the ocean. As I reflect back, I don't think that is quite true. Dominion was shared by ocean and forest, but we were more aware of the former because of its movement. The forest was more obstinate, if not as potent. It was very difficult to penetrate. I found that the ground cover was tricky. In jumping from a log into thick vegetation, I allowed for the same distance to the ground I would encounter in the Smokies. Often I found I would plunge a foot deeper and would lose my balance and composure. The ocean, serenely going through the slow pulsations of its tides through those three days, seemed more friendly.

But those detached knobs and cylinders and battlements of rock rising out of the sea and the disintegrating necks of soil

133

and rock which tied others of the knobs to the land gave quiet evidence of its ruthless power. Someone asked whether I thought the ocean was moving inland. Those knobs of rock, standing like ghostly buildings and observatories in the shifting fog, must once have been a part of the land. Now they were out to sea, their feet in the tides and their sides lashed and ground by the storms. But some retained jaunty halos and headdresses of their former estate. Some had toupees of low growing shrubs and others a rakish tree or two sprouting bravely from a fissure. I think those grasses and trees were vestiges — precarious evidences — of the landed ancestry of these knobs. Many of them were bleak and bare, their foundations the languorous resting places of sea lions. These we saw several times in considerable numbers, supine and lazy on low wave-swept reefs.

But over the short view, forest and sea had fought to a draw. In some places the high tide came within a few feet of the matted forest, which seemed to be holding its own even against the terrible power of the storms. Perhaps the points caught the full fury of the gales, whereas the shelving beaches rolled with the storms and blunted their power. I would be foolish to say, after one visit, which is ascendant just now.

We hurried our steps to catch those rocky points at low tide. The saddles we crossed on a couple of occasions were not too difficult. Perhaps on an ocean hike, it was simply unthinkable to take to the land. Perhaps we enjoyed the little game with the waves — the hesitation on a knob above the water while the wave ebbed and gave us a chance to advance. But if it were more sporting, it was a game with an edge, because one of the Justice's friends, an elderly man, who had come up from La Push to meet us, had been caught by a wave, alone and unprotected on one of those exposed ledges, and had

134

barely escaped with his life. So there was need for caution and good sense in this little game we played with the sea. These considerations moved us to get up in the damp and eerie fog of the pre-dawn for a race with the tide to one of these jutting and hazardous ribs of rock.

Our hike down the coast was more like a painting than a play. It was an experience of great beauty, but not an experience of great events or situations. Nothing really exciting happened except the mild excitement provided by new scenes and new people. There was stimulation enough in watching the endless panorama. There was stimulus in exchanging ideas with new people. I felt drawn to Vic Scheffer, the scientist, quiet and reserved, with a great knowledge of some of our notable sea mammals.

The scenes of the panorama overlapped. The sweet fragrance of the dying bracken, the great spruces and firs merging into the fog were a part of the landscape and yet somehow withdrawn from it. The acres and acres of tawny cobbles made treacherous by kelp — the chalky drift logs, the stark, rocky points, gendarmes and outposts — the little coves and the offshore islands huddled in the fog — the level beaches of light, coffee-colored sand — the transparent film and spindrift of a spent wave — the rolling blue waves breaking into dazzling white — the gorgeous reflections of a beach saturated with water — the regal frown of a bald eagle surveying us from a dead fir high above the beach — the colorful wizardry of a sunset overpouring beach and rocks and water — the startling colors of things of the sea — the green of the anemones, the purple of the sea urchins and the salmon-pink of the starfish — a walk across flat ledges with barnacles exploding under our feet

135

— the unbelievable transparencies of the tidal pools deep in the ledges — tiny human figures bent under their packs walking alone, silhouetted against the fog or the sea — all these were the shifting scenes and overlapping vignettes of the ocean hike.

The last day moved to a kind of climax. Under Douglas's restless prodding, we arose from the fragrant bracken as the stronger light of day touched the waning blue light of the moon. People were getting used to the early rising and I suspect that by now many were stirred by the freshness and hush of the early dawn. Nearly everyone was under way by 6:30. Again we lurched across long beaches of gigantic cobbles. Again we pressed to pass a rocky notch ahead of the mounting tide. Once we looked down from a stony out-crop onto the swirling after-tow of a wave. It was lit by the fog-muted sun into molten bronze. Dim figures, moving around its edges, looked like Vulcan's men. Over a level beach, saturated with water, we moved across reflections of ourselves, and seemed to be suspended in mid-air between the over-arching bowl of the sky and an under-arching bowl of the sea.

Ultimately we came to a glorious beach which was firm and inviting. To the south it was blocked by a wall of rock which nosed into the sea. A hole in that wall, a kind of needle's eye, was our objective before noon. When the waves started racing through that eye we would be held until the late, late afternoon unless we chose to climb across a crumbling neck of loose earth and briers as we had done earlier. Near noon we threaded this barrier and had lunch just beyond. This was the Rialto Beach, a stupendous place. Great monoliths of rock, as large as a skyscraper, were all about. Beyond them was an incredibly flat and firm beach, the color of deeply weathered boards. It was

136

beautiful and exotic, a wide avenue, narrowing before the tide, between a continent to the east of us and the Pacific to the west.

Here we needed no direction. The inevitability of our route was part of the charm. To our left were the dense, brier-choked, hardly-penetrable virgin woods; on our right the sweeping expanse of the Pacific. Under intelligent guidance, we had hardly been aware of the narrowness of our route, squeezed between land and sea. We had passed all but one of those constrictions, where land and sea met, without being aware of it. And we came out at the high tides upon curving sandy coves which were roomy and ample, except in the booming terror of a storm.

Finally after lunch we tramped barefooted on the healing sand, past the last great monolith onto a loose kaleidoscope of rainbowed pebbles. We were met by a man with a tape recorder who was surrounded by a knot of people gathered just a hundred yards distant from the roadhead. At the roadhead were concentrated the destroyers of uniqueness and of individuality — the ubiquitous common denominator of our twentieth century civilization, the automobile.

The scenes were mighty as we walked along this remnant beach, the meeting place of earth and sea — wild, untamed, and tremendous.

PARK CREEK PASS
CASCADE PASS
WASHINGTON
1958

THE WILDERNESS Society Council and friends met under a pall at Stehekin, Washington — a pall of smoke which reddened the moon and the sun, and a pall of anxiety and concern that the forest fires on the opposite slopes of the North Cascades would get out of hand. The fire threat became so severe on Monday night we were advised that the Forest Service was going to "close" the forest and that our field trip was off. The next morning about noon we were advised that there had been a change in the weather and that we might go as planned.

PARK CREEK PASS

In the morning, in moisture and light rain, all of us wore ponchos as we rode the topless bus twenty miles up the Stehekin Gorge in the North Cascades to the mouth of Park Creek. It was exciting. The forests were dense, and the gorge was deep and the stream-flow great. The gravel road went steadily up from one thousand feet at Stehekin to perhaps twenty-five hundred feet at the horse camp. Twice the turns were so sharp, the long bus had to be backed up in order to get around them. The mist blew in my face, and it was welcome after the scorching, smoky days and nights at the lodge.

There were the usual delays in en-horsing. Some of us walked up the river to a spot where the whole Stehekin River was crammed between rock walls not ten feet apart. Although principally glacial water, the silt had settled out and the stream seemed green and clear as it raced between the walls.

After the slow process of adjusting people to horses, and saddles to people, we started out in single file through a forest of giant Douglas firs and western cedars. Because of their beautiful symmetry I wasn't aware, until we came back to the Smokies, how large those trees really were. There were ferns and bracken. Once we saw maidenhair ferns. We rode over a ridge before dropping into Park Creek and the vistas were rugged and beetling.

We went by easy stages with two long rests. Our packers were considerate of horses and of men. It was probably steeper country than any we had been in, except possibly in the Cloud Peak area.

Crossing the unbridged creek, we rode through awesome groves, then through thickets of willows. Drooping clouds blocked out all views for a time. But as we took to the right slope, following short, sharp switchbacks, we suddenly became aware of the prodigious and frightening wall of the opposite slope. It was so precipitous it seemed top-heavy. Spots of snow and glaciers gave rise to almost vertical streams which boomed down the slopes — white, living threads amidst the somber rock

139

and trees. And up the main valley, the darkened fog lifted to show dirty glaciers, and dark pyramids which reached gauntly into the clouds.

The switchbacks were punishing. Brandy criticized them sharply, saying they were too steep and were hard on horses and an invitation to erosion.

At near six thousand feet, the forest became sparse and dwarfed and we went through beautiful shrubby mountain ash, which sparkled with orange berries. Then we crossed a couple of small streams bedecked with blooms of the Grass of Parnassus — a more spindly and less showy variety than the *P. asarifolia* of the Smokies. We then emerged upon the tundral meadow of the camping area.

The cook tent used by the Sierra Club was still there — a green box-like affair with a large fly, and two wood-burning, and one gas-burning, camp stoves. We had hot drinks while awaiting the pack horses and then fanned out onto some timbered knolls with commanding views of the valley to locate campsites.

Anne and I picked a level spot near some small evergreens which I thought would give us shelter from the wind. This spot broke precipitously downward about twenty feet to the west of us and again one hundred feet to the south. It was a sort of promontory projecting out from the main area of tundra and fairly overhung the valley. It was a tremendous place and we were to find that this was a very exposed place and that wind and rain would tear into us from every point of the compass.

The moon was nearly full. Clouds swept before it and then passed on. An improbably steep wall rose three thousand feet above us to the east. In the night the clouds whipped between us and the wall, obscuring it in white mystery. Then the moon

140

would shine out and whiten the wall with an eerie light. Rain, wind, clouds, and moonlight followed in wild succession. I never tired of the awesome whitening of the east wall and I was never sure in the tumultuous vagaries of the night whether it was fog or moonlight which raced across it. Once we got up and I stood shivering at the edge of our precipice listening to the violence of the wind and watching the sweep of cloud and moonlight patterns through the shadowed gulf of the valley. I would have liked to watch it for hours, as I had watched the aurora on Crackshot Lake two years ago, but was driven back to my sleeping bag by my chattering teeth and shivering body. A wild uproarious night in the land of the glaciers!

In the pre-dawn, I roused and shook myself fully awake. There was a breath of color in the narrow V of the valley. I dressed and, taking my camera, set off across the moors, following a deep path up a steep, grassy slope. A rounded rib of white rock on which there were scattered pine and spruces shut off my view of the glaciers. I scrambled breathlessly up its side. Grass and scattered trees stretched along this rib which extended a quarter of a mile parallel to the main axis of the valley. Beyond it were the glaciers — wrinkled and grimy and with the faintest cast of blue. The sun was fitful. Little color — few beams. The ledge was as sharp as a roof, and I moved rapidly from one side to the other for views. There were massive whitebark pines, tapering spruce, and fragile, golden tamarack. The glaciers clung to the lip of the steep, rounded cup at the head of the valley. Two skeins of water pounded down through gray talus filling the air with a sustained roar. Black pyramids of rock rose above the sprawling glaciers, their summits lost in swirling mist. It was a wild, gaunt, and booming scene — as austere and thunderous as anything I had experienced.

141

To the east and far below me, I picked out our sleeping promontory. Reluctantly I descended the grassy shelves and vertical deer trails to the cook tent for breakfast.

I had no real forewarning of the vastness, nor of the cruel ruggedness of the area. We had visualized a kind of rolling, rounded summit along which we could move without too much exertion to nearby spots. Of course I had not reckoned with the heavy fog which lay over all the peaks during the three days we were amongst them. Nor had I reckoned with the ever-recurring precipices. Everywhere there was steepness and unscalable walls. One ridge back of camp, rocky and grassy and exposed, seemed to offer some possibilities.

It was a good day. There was much sunshine although the highest peaks never fully emerged from the clouds. This ridge also commanded the glaciers and the upper part of the valley, and being higher than the one we were on in the morning provided massive views. It had no timber. The ridge was above timber line, and was made up of outcroppings of light gray rock, and benches and shelves of good turf. We traveled in the open. There were tremendous views every foot of the way. This ridge led to the main divide, which was much higher than Park Creek Pass.

Bernie and I found a small cairn on top, and the summit seemed to be joined by a rocky ridge to Mt. Booker. We were on the main divide of the North Cascades. Fog lay densely to the north of us. But to the south there was a prodigious vista of glacial valleys and serrated peaks.

The great events of this day came on the descent. G. M. and Stewart Brandborg had lingered on an outcrop of rock which commanded the entire east wall, festooned with cliffs and

142

ravines, talus slopes, scarred areas of raw earth, and grassy benches. With the binoculars they had spotted a nannie, a yearling, and a kid of the mountain goat, grazing across one of the grassy shelves. I could see the animals easily with the glasses — the tiny pointed horns and the coat of white hair. I had seen goats before, but in this vast wilderness setting, the sight of them provided a great thrill.

Vertically below us on a bench of talus and grass, Brandy senior pointed out some birds — a mottled gray, slightly smaller than pheasants. These were ptarmigan, unbelievably tame. Bernie and I went down amongst them and took photographs almost at will. It was one of my few experiences with wildlife that had no fear of man. This was surely wilderness!

On the second night the air was distinctly cooler — in the upper thirties. Neither the packers nor the Brandborgs would venture a prediction as to what the night would bring. I felt positive that it was too cold to rain. But I was a prophet away from home.

It was one of the wilder nights I have spent in the outdoors. Nothing really happened. We were not cold — the minimum was only 36°. We didn't get drenched — but we were cramped and damp. Our tarp, pitched on a slant, was about four feet high at our heads and eighteen inches at our feet. Its dimensions were roughly seven by fourteen feet. When pitched at an angle, it barely covered a person lying crosswise to its long axis. All sides were open. It was stretched as tightly as I could make it, but with no stakes, my anchors were large stones which moved a little under pressure. Some of the ties were thongs and some were cotton cords. The thongs tended to stretch. Hence our tarp sagged just a little, and the wind, roaring in, moved under it

143

and would belly it up like a sail and pop it like a whip. This went on for hours. The wind shook our tarp like a terrier with a snake. Pop-pop, pop — and with the wind came rain, not a deluge, but hard. It blew under. We first realized our feet were catching the drip at the bottom of the tarp. We pulled in our feet and lay cramped and strained. Then the rain began pouring in at our heads and we took our ponchos and covered our heads. The rain, which the ponchos caught, drained down between our air mattresses. Sometimes when the wind was stilled, the water collected in the swag of the tarp and I would empty it with a great splashing. It was a wild, roaring, noisy, and dampish night — and yet we have been wetter many times in the Smokies. But the awesome cliffs and the nearby glaciers placed this storm in a bleaker environment than the Smokies.

The next morning, hovering in ponchos, we arose in the rain, ate in the crowded cook tent, packed in the rain and stored our luggage in a pile under a scanty tarp.

Later, in a driving rain, George Marshall and I took down the tent used by the Brandborgs. Water collected by the gallon in every low place. Ropes were wet and were tied to evergreens which were wetter than sponges. Our arms got wet as we pulled at the ropes and folded the tent; our glasses became fogged. We finally got the tent folded and slithered down the muddy path with fifty pounds of weight between us.

I was never really disturbed. Only our hands were cold, and only our extremities were wet. The packers, without oilskins, were warm in their heavy woolens and seemed least perturbed of all. This was in the day's work for them. They worked easily and good humoredly, even clowning with the horses, when one of them "spooked" at an old charred stump.

The place where we had camped was near-level tundra with

a terrific cliff on the east and rounded ridges rolling up to high ledges. There were scattered trees above us, but essentially we were at timber line. It was a spacious place which terminated in rocky talus or ledges in every direction except down. There was some turf, but it was scant in depth and in the rain was quickly churned into greasy, treacherous slime. The paths, all worn through to the soil, were slick and slimy. The area around the tent was not littered. It had been commendably policed by the Sierra Club, but it was worn. The cliffs were unusable and these level highlands, although giving a sense of ampleness, were too cramped for large parties. Wilderness has to be big to preserve its character at timber line.

Ultimately the horses were all packed and we mounted them onto wet saddles. The lower we went, the lighter the rain. And when we reached the heavy timber, the seemingly muddy trails were speedily kicked into dust.

The trail down was hung on a near-vertical slope. Once I looked back, where Jack was leading the pack horses. There were ten in the string. The trail was winding so tightly those ten horses in the string were moving in four directions!

We edged through willows and, almost imperceptibly, into the great forest. It seemed so natural. Up high there was rugged scenery, cliffs, bare upland, glaciers, clouds, black peaks, and vertical streams. Here in the friendlier valley the great trees took over, throwing a mantle of appropriateness over the gentler slopes. These were massive trees, bulky at the base but so slimly tapering they belied their huge proportions. Anne and I became so used to them we took them for granted until, crossing the Smokies two weeks later, their after-image made the eastern forest trees seem tiny by comparison.

Everything — mountains and forest — had been on such a

145

giant scale that, with nothing to compare them, we had lost perspective. The country had an unsurpassed grandeur and amplitude — nothing in any direction but sharpened peaks and glaciers and the U-shaped canyons with their lining of forest. The forest belonged to the tundra and cliffs, and the tundra and cliffs set off the forest. Each edged into the other naturally and appropriately. Out of the cover of the trees the naked grandeur of the high country burst upon us. And out of the exposed upland, we dropped gradually into the peace of the forest. The august gentleness of the forest framed and contained the stark immensity of the cliffs and glaciers.

In a colonnade of herculean firs we pitched our tarp for the third night. Full moon and soft clouds vied for space in the deep boundless blue, and we slept grandly, and without disturbance under the calm of the forest.

CASCADE PASS

The next morning with Marty and Peter, the two junior packers, and David Simons, Anne and I rode up the main valley of the Stehekin to Cascade Pass. This valley was narrow also. A Paul Bunyan could have stood in the creek and touched the walls on either side. Deep side canyons opened off from it like nuggets on a chain, including Surprise Lake and Horseshoe Canyon with its curtain of waterfalls. The floor of the main valley was torn and gutted — mining. A road had been gouged through the vegetation to the unstable talus, which lay raw and barren to the eye. And the willows and other trees of this north country were trying to pick up the raveled web and tie this land together again with a fabric of roots. A flood had torn out the road and probably wiped out the mine up in Horseshoe Canyon.

Violence begat violence and the results were here for all to see.

The trail followed what was left of the road, and then departed from it to take off across the shifting repose of an enormous talus slope. No grading, no footing — just a slight rearrangement of the loose stones. Even the rearrangement would be lost to us a hundred feet ahead. Over this the horses stumbled and clattered, and when we dismounted they followed us gratefully as we led them across this shifting nightmare. Eventually we came to some mountain ash and vine maples, growing incongruously out of this rocky waste, to which they gave color and a measure of linkage. As we rounded the head of the valley we glanced across at a vertical ravine down which tossed the thread of a stream which seemed to be falling out of the low-lying clouds. On our side, the loose talus gave way to solid cliff, and the clinking rocks to crusty gravel. We climbed across the face of the valley on a narrow shelf to which increasing vegetation gave a false sense of security. And then we read a sign which stripped away our calm:

> DISMOUNT AND LEAD YOUR HORSES
> FOR THE NEXT QUARTER OF A MILE

Through a screen of saplings, we looked down almost terrified into misty depths a thousand feet below. We emerged upon a forested ridge of towering firs. Near the top of this nightmare valley and between the ancient paths of the glaciers these great trees had found lodgment and grew to gigantic size. Long skeins of greenish gray moss hung from their limbs and gave a weird unreality to the violence about us. We ate in their shelter, as the clouds condensed in their tops. In mist and dampness and gloom, and in the chill from the unseen glaciers, we relaxed while the horses grazed on the thin grass.

We pushed on along a faint wavering trail and then across the insecurity of more talus to the cloud-girt Cascade Pass. Here again we found an uneasy sod finding lodgment amid outpost trees. A road pushed up on the west side within a mile and a half of the top, and several hiking and camping parties had erected tiny camps in the wind-swept trees. It was a damp, unkempt, over-used and littered place, and we quickly took it in and returned to our horses and led them downward to the cleaner violence of the lower valley.

We never saw the glaciers nor the surrounding peaks — only the low, close-packed fog. It was a day of unrealized expectation — the torn lower valley and trampled pass bespoke all too clearly the precariousness of this country — and the need for a settled policy to contain and preserve it.

15

THE BLUE Range Primitive Area in the Apache National
Forest in eastern Arizona looked bad to me. There was
little grass, and we could see eroding fingers of bare soil through
the brush on opposing slopes. We saw occasional gullies a yard
deep and a yard across taking shape within a hundred feet of
the top of a ridge. Why was this classified as a primitive area?
What gave it its wilderness quality?

We used horses here. The country was rough. In some of the
savannas, a jeep would have found easy going, but around a
place like Sissy Point, or down the precipitous slopes of the
North Fork of the Blue River and in the fickle meanders of the
trail from right to left bank, and from left to right bank, and
down the flood plains of loose gravel and stone, a jeep could
not have traveled. We were forced by the ruggedness of the
country to use the simplest feasible means of travel —
horseback.

Most of the scant rainfall emanated from the Gulf of Mexico. But by the time the clouds reached Arizona they had been pretty well wrung out and there was not much water left in them.

The chief influence on the physical·environment, and a very damaging one, was the cattle. There had been overgrazing for decades and the grass and browse had become thinner and thinner. There was a harsh barrenness to many of the lower ridges, even though distant views were not unbeautiful.

This was one of my few experiences with vertical-sided canyons cutting into a mesa-like plateau. I wasn't too much aware of them until we emerged upon an escarpment overlooking the Blue River itself. It was a scene of gray and green — gray cliffs and gray walls and green trees and grass treading the valley and clinging flatly to the mesa above. In the deepening twilight the canyons were sharply etched and I felt that here was something different. The Blue River was clear — its flow, placid and scant. Water is the life of this country — any country for that matter — but one is hardly aware of this until he goes through land where water is scarce.

Originating and living as I do in the rainy southeast, the hot, arid, and treeless deserts of the southwest have fascinated me. But many of them have seemed impenetrable and hopeless, and I have been rebuffed by what I saw.

Great spaces seem synonymous with richness. I am wondering if understanding of the limitations of this land and restraint in its use may not do something for it. I suppose I but scratch the surface in understanding the ecology, much less the economics, of the area.

The memories I carry most vividly from that Arizona visit are of the forests of ponderosa pine. Those sturdy magnificent

150

trees with warm, russet deeply-plated bark gave a sense of well being. They are perhaps not as shapely as the redwoods or the great spruces and firs, but they have a rugged down-to-earth quality which I loved. The larger the trees, the greater the openness between, and the longer and more inviting the vistas. This was savanna country at its best — with beckoning reaches of grass stretching in every direction. One could ride almost at will through such country.

On Black Mountain the long summit gave little feeling of being the top of a mountain. Because the horse trail threaded the center of the ridge, there were flat expanses on either side as far as we could see. Of course, when we started up the final knob the slopes were steep, and there were sharp switchbacks from which we obtained mountain-top views which extended across the forested ridges to sun-baked plateaus and deserts. It was a gigantic prospect which glimmered under a desert sun.

To the north we saw the green gash along the Blue River, and dry harsh castellated canyons and outcrops beyond. All my life I had heard of box canyons. From the eyrie of the Black Mountain fire tower we saw several. It was a tremendous view.

No one can claim that the Blue Range Primitive Area is first-class land. It has variety, and some of it is superlatively scenic. But it has been tragically overused. The vegetation, clinging stubbornly to thin soils, is starved for water. Even the forests which seem to tower grandly above the struggles of the grasses and animals beneath would be the richer for more care. But it is country with a powerful, if subtle, appeal, and except for the one stub road down the Blue River is devoid of roads. Harsh and rugged though it be, it rests the spirit. One senses the great cycles of weather and growth, erosion and resurgence. The noisy nervousness of the motor age is absent and one begins to feel a larger rhythm and contentment. One feels there the majestic pulse of the natural world to which most men ultimately respond. It is the antithesis of the world of clocks and schedules and target dates.

There we found freedom and expansiveness. Maybe some people get a feeling of expansiveness in riding through a forest in a car. For those individuals it is better than nothing. The deeps of experience are not reached until one has committed himself to the wilds, the weather, the winds, and the unrestrained beauties. It has been stated well in the objectives of the Wilderness Bill. Thin as it was, the Blue Range Primitive Area, far beyond the havens of man, offered all these things.

Winds! I think I have never heard the music of the pines rendered with greater volume or compulsion than in the ponderosas of Arizona. There were surges so powerful that one had the sense they were irresistible. One became keyed to some climax of momentous import. And then came the slow decline and a bare fingering of the needles in the tree tops. There was a rhythm which made one think of the endless procession of waves against the shore. But it was on a grander scale, more like the tides, like day following the night. And there was mystery. The long surges could not be seen like the break of a wave on the sands. One did not anticipate them as he does the breakers. For the winds he waited. His spirit tingled. Will it come again? And then far off, like a ballad meant to be overheard and not heard, he sensed the soft forerunner. Then the inexorable, gradual build up to a full-throated climax which tended to tear needle from twig, twig from limb, and limb from tree.

16

SALMON RIVER
BIG HORN CRAGS
IDAHO
1960

W E FOLLOWED the Salmon River by car downstream about eighteen miles to Shoup, Idaho. Even in the late summer doldrums, the river was swift and strong, and the mountains sharply rising on either side were rugged. It was easy to see why the Lewis and Clark scouts had turned back after descending this canyon a few miles and had sought out the more inviting route up the North Fork. History does not disclose just how far they proceeded down the Salmon before its austerities overwhelmed them. But their expedition was to trade the burning heat and cliffs of the Salmon River for the paralyzing snows of the Lolo Trail, where a few days later they floundered horse-belly deep through drifts. The struggles of Lewis and Clark through this violent country were becoming ever more real.

154

Below Shoup the Salmon slipped swiftly down a steady gradient. The water was at the seasonal low and I saw none of the great waves for which it is notorious. But the canyon extended sixty miles beyond the terminus of our road, and undoubtedly there was rough water farther down. This day the gorge was blisteringly hot, and the farther down we drove the more furnace-like the crags alongside.

We went perhaps twenty miles below Pine Creek and were perhaps thirty or forty miles below the mouth of the North Fork of the Salmon. In that distance the honey-colored ridges of grass gave way to gaunt sterile cliffs. We had views of perpendicular battlements from the suspension bridge where we got our last glimpse down river. The surrounding peaks rose to 9600 feet. Shoup was but 3400 feet. It is quite possible, as Brandy has suggested, that it is the deepest canyon in the country and one of the longest.

Curiously, when we drove out of the canyon to go to the Long Tom Lookout on the north rim, we ran through a belt of excellent ponderosa pine. Moisture conditions were modified by the elevation and conducive to the growth of timber. The trees thinned out as we went higher. There was no snow and not too much water. Eventually we emerged upon a bleak, rocky promontory across which poured a chilling wind. This spot was on the rim of the canyon although the river could be seen at only one point. It was a tremendous mountain scene! Bleakness, ruggedness, and mass spread in every direction as far as the eye could see. Across the river we looked into the Salmon River Breaks; to the west and north, into the great Selway-Bitterroot wilderness. To the east we saw the snowy pyramids of the Continental Divide. We could see the tiny pimples of a half dozen fire lookouts.

Bill Zimmerman looked at it for a long time and then said wryly, "Even our opponents would say, 'What use is it except for wilderness.' " I hope he is right. Snow lies deep in the winter and the temperature gets down to 40° below and stays uniformly so. What country!

But there were a few in-holdings. A placer mine on a tributary of Panther Creek muddied that creek to its mouth on the Salmon and influenced the color of the Salmon itself for several miles down stream. On the upper Panther were the closed-down works of a cobalt mine. In operation, we were told, the effluent therefrom was an inky black – and both banks were seared free of vegetation for a yard or more above low water flow.

BIG HORN CRAGS

On our way into the Big Horn Crags all roads were dusty and gravelly, with forbidding grades, and constantly mounting elevations. Even the approach to the area of the crags was something to remember.

From the packers' road camp we followed a short cut along a little stream which speedily gave out, and emerged upon the final gritty mile of the road. Beyond the roadhead the first mile of the trail was harsh and rocky. Some of it wound precariously over living rock. Below it was a cirque and rock wall as steep and blank as Half Dome. But as we plodded upward through a sketchy forest, we began to see fantastic outcroppings of rock. They were gray and orange and tan, and were pitted with bowl-like cavities which merged into each other in fascinating patterns. These masses of alien rock were huge – fifty, a hundred, two hundred feet high, emerging like monuments on the crest of the ridge we were following. One of the most massive and striking rose hundreds of feet above the granite ridge which there formed the boundary of the Idaho Primitive Area. It was a kind of monument country. One of the rangers said the crags were batholiths. But if these crags were once intruded rock, the granite rock had eroded down from around them leaving them stark and exposed and giving the whole locale a unique and flinty majesty.

One was aware of this pervasive aridness whether he rode or walked. Walking or riding, a small cloud of dust accompanied us like an aura. On foot I kicked it up around my ankles. On horseback, I moved in the advancing swirl of dust which accompanied our party. We were slated to camp on the shores of Welcome Lake. We did camp in the forest about a half mile below, where there was more room, more firewood, and less danger of depredation from a she-bear which had slashed to ribbons one tent at Welcome Lake, reputedly because someone had shot her cub. Our campsite was a pleasant place with a rounded monolith on one side, the stream on two others, and a view of a nice, rocky ravine and waterfall from the cook tent. On the fourth side and downstream was a boggy meadow which was fanned with small rivulets flowing down from the surrounding ridges.

George and I decided to walk up to Welcome Lake. I was not exhausted, but I was very tired, and attributed it to the elevation, about eight thousand feet. The lake pleased me. Here was water and a nice snow slope or two above it. It had an irregular shape and there were pleasing vistas in several directions. But the water flow was not great and the turf was boggy near the outlet. Even in this remote place the grass was

157

thin and sparse from overcamping and overgrazing. We saw no cattle; overgrazing here was from pack stock.

The next day Bernie Frank, Ernest Griffith and I started from camp a few minutes before nine with the Terrace Lakes as our objective. But the skies began to clear and by the time we reached a fork in the trail (a place of decision) we had a huddle and decided to try for McGuire Peak. It was a lucky judgment. By changing our plans, we entered upon several hours of stirring and exhilarating exploration. Before departing we left a note conspicuously on a tree to acquaint the others with our intentions.

Ernest had the map. Our route appeared to be up the slopes of the divide which here formed the boundary of the Primitive Area and thence along the divide to the offshoot ridge which led to McGuire. Immediately, we attempted to follow a disappearing animal trail in a shallow drainage which we hoped would take us to the vicinity of Harbor and Wilson Lakes. The trail was poor and although there were some blazes, they were not consecutive. From below, we had no perspective, and found that the lake basins were always over another rolling bench on this granite mountain.

There was some confusion also from the crags. We were not among them. Bernie thought one on the south was Cathedral Rock, although I thought the one in question was on a side ridge. A near ridge hid the terrain, and when we worked beyond its dominance, we realized we were nowhere near the lakes and far below the divide. But we were getting higher and into a thin, grassy upland with colossal granite boulders and outcrops. The slope was still climbable but we ascended the meadow by a flanking approach. I was behind taking pictures. The others suddenly waved their arms and whooped. They had spotted

158

four mountain sheep strung out on a ledge above us. They were hardly more than a hundred yards away and seemed to be aware of us, but unexcited. One was smaller than the others, three ewes and a lamb. They moved casually along this grassy, rocky ledge.

We were getting into rough country, and remembering our trip with the Muries on Sheep Mountain in Wyoming, I began to look with concern for the trail of the sheep. So far we had been able to pick our way easily along wide shelves and grassy benches. But there was still no lake. We had thought it would be in the narrow pocket from which we had first glimpsed the sheep.

With some doing, we came to a fringe of trees and Ernest said, "Harbor Lake." Below it on the map was Wilson Lake and it was our hope to cross between them in our drive for the crest. We drifted to the right, came to the end of the lake and found a yawning gulf below us. I began to have my doubts, since the map indicated that the two lakes were close together. Bernie studied the map and said its shape was not right for Harbor Lake. Ernest conceded reluctantly. We were already retracing our steps through the screen of timber along the water's edge, when we heard riders from the camp. One of the foresters confirmed that we were on Wilson Lake and not Harbor Lake. So we worked to the upper end of Wilson Lake and took off on a steep, grassy meadow around the edge. Then through a fringe of trees, an enormous pocket opened and we saw the longer Harbor Lake.

The pitch of the ledges above the lakes was dangerous. We thought we could see our course, but I was still looking for the sheep trail since we had seen the sheep once again above Wilson

159

Lake. We had now come to a calico pattern of grass and loose rock. On the crest high above were two giant crags. We set out on a tilted bench of vegetation and hoped to find a way up to and between the crags. Here we climbed very rapidly. The lakes shimmered in the sun beneath us.

We three were on our own in the home country of the bighorn sheep. The grass shelf merged into the slope of the mountain and dwindled out. A gnarled and twisted ponderosa clung to this slope, through whose limbs we could see the dancing sparkle of Wilson Lake almost straight down.

I sat down and when I did so, I coasted an inch or two on loose gravel. The footing was so loose and precipitous it began to roll under us and we reached out with our hands for added support. This was exhilarating, but it was not fun. There was no firm sheep path; there was a sharp gradient with loose granite barely in repose.

We started up again, on all fours, clinging to scattered tussocks of grass. I found myself terribly exposed on unstable talus, with a cliff at the drop-off point. Bernie had found a rib of rock about twenty feet to the left. It was highly fractured and strewn with loose stones. I inched across the talus slope to this uncertain rib and clung for a moment slightly disturbed and completely breathless. Looking down we could see Ernest's head and shoulders only, as he looked up at us. We clung to whatever we could − a rigid tableaux of three in brilliant sunshine. One of the rangers had said that he once rode a horse across the divide in this vicinity. But we were sure no horse had ever scratched its way up this route.

Bernie was above me. He angled to the right for the protection of some scrawny timber. I inched up the outcrop and followed a wedge of grass across the slope to the friendly timber. In doing so I crossed the trunk of a fallen tree and wondered dreamily if my added weight would pull it loose. It didn't.

We were now near the crest. The slope eased and we scrambled to the dubious safety of the top. On that frightening climb, we had almost forgotten Mt. McGuire but as I stood erect and caught my breath, I took one look and said,

"We can't make it."

We were safely on the summit all right, but those grim, unclimbable crags protruded like the plates on the back of a stegosaurus all along the main divide which we had now reached. We were in the shadow of one which overhung us to the east, two hundred feet above. There was a series of them to the west. The slope in front of us dropped dizzily to Clear Lake, a thousand feet below.

We were safe, momentarily. But none of us relished returning by that patchwork of rolling rock and flimsy grass by which we had ascended. And the slope which dropped at our feet seemed worse. No grass, nothing but massive slopes of snow and rock chunks. Ernest joined us. Bernie worked to the left and returned discouraged. We were about to try a slanting traverse to the east, which we agreed ended in a monumental uncertainty. There were drop-offs below and huge swells in the talus which concealed our possible course. We had gotten into our predicament together and consulted on every move, pooling our knowledge, fears, and uncertainties. Cahalane writes that "ledges, cliffs, and steep slopes of broken rock" mean greater safety for the bighorn sheep. But we were mere men, two-footed, with no suction cups on our feet, and we were worried.

Just before we took off, I asked the others to hold up a

minute while I worked over to the base of the great crag to the east of us. One glance and I said,

"Here's our route." Along its base the fragmented rock lay in a narrow shelf against the monolith. Ernest asked rather sharply, "Are you sure?"

And I was sure, except that I couldn't see all the way to a timbered ridge which jutted to the north a quarter of a mile away. But so far as I could see, it was safer than the terriby exposed talus upon which we had been about to enter.

Bernie agreed and we took off. No rocks rolled under us. If they had, we might have broken a leg, or most certainly lacerated our hides on their jagged edges. We were doing all right and moving with ease. Then we came to a terrifying heap of stones, which were so steeply piled against the base of the crag, we were afraid we would set them adrift by our own weight.

We consulted again. I thought we could work down, away from the base of the crag, and below that particular pile to a point where the slope seemed to offer more stability. We all agreed, but as we descended we saw a drop-off below us. Beyond it was a tiny knife edge of rock with a few scrawny trees which also seemed to end in a cliff. We *were* in a dilemma. I inched over to a steeply lying snow slope. It seemed crusty and safe. I thought I could kick holes in it, and tried a few. Ernest didn't like this, but it seemed our only route. It was two hundred feet across. It was crusted, but had melted just a trifle, and seemed granular and safe. Even so, its pitch was so steep, I dug my bare fingers into the snow up to my palms at each step. Bernie followed. I came to another roll in the slope. I paused to look back. Bernie and Ernest were clinging almost like flies to the snow and I could see the thread of a trail we had stitched across it with our feet.

Again we had a decision to make. There was a little hollow to cross where the grade was steeper before we reached the timbered ridge. I thought we should ascend a bit and cross a smaller snow field to the base of the crag. This rock was even more unstable, and we had some tense moments, but it was the key and we emerged at last on firm soil. This patch of soil merged into a continuous, craggy ridge with timber scattered along it.

According to the map the trail crossed this ridge at its north end and since the rock was massive and firm under our feet, we decided to follow along its crest to the trail.

Ernest asked the time. I said, "Eleven thirty."

He said, "You are kidding." So great had been our concentration on the worst of the upgrade and on the whole of the descent to this point, it had seemed like many hours. Actually we had lived days in a relatively few tense minutes. We were now relaxed. We could look down, almost as though we were hanging over it, into the depths of the upper of the Clear Lakes. We could look southeast to the steep switchbacks below Beaver Slide Pass. We could look southwest to the appallingly steep course we had followed across snow and talus. We looked farther to the west beyond a series of smaller crags set in the main divide to a slope of scree which descended to the very edge of Clear Lake. Had we been able to go west instead of east when we reached the divide, we could have descended those thousand feet of scree in complete safety in a matter of minutes. We were now far enough around to see that the small tempting spine of timber which had first beckoned to us earlier would have ended in an unclimbable cliff.

We ate and decided to follow the ridge to the trail and the

trail along the shore of the upper Clear Lake and climb the divide again at a saddle where we could look over at Airplane and Ship Island Lakes. Our day was not over, but we knew we would have no more such hours as we had just been through.

We had some good moments on the tremendous rounded stones which were strung along the backbone of this ridge. We could have had some tense ones had we decided to drop off the west side to Clear Lake. But we didn't, and contented ourselves with looking deep into it from above. Its waters were not quite clear. It was a baffling robin's-egg blue with deeper shadows where boulders lay near the surface. It was not clear like the streams although it had a sparkling clarity when we drank from it a half hour later. We worked down through the trees on the east slope and missed an easy ramp of talus on the west which was quite evident as we later looked back at it from the lake.

From the ridge we had observed the zigzagging ladder-like steepness of the trail to Beaver Slide Pass which we were to follow later. It had some snow on it, and when we churned up its slope at the end of the day, water was seeping down the gravelly trough which served as a trail.

Down at the lake we hunted a stone upon which to prop ourselves while we drank. A small frog scrambled away from my face. In such a place, I felt kinship with him. This was his world, not mine. I was enjoying it for fleeting moments and I did not question his prior right to be there. The little meadow, by which we approached the lake and from which we obtained fine vistas to the boundary wall we had just descended, was studded with short indigo-blue gentians. They were the blue of the midnight sky, and amidst the tawny meadow were scattered about with the approximate frequency of stars in the sky.

164

Disdaining the trail in this open country, we set a straight course from the lake to the low point in the boundary of the Primitive Area. The gap itself was thickly covered with small trees. There was a tiny open meadow to the south, whence we obtained commanding views into this drainage. Mt. McGuire and its approach ridge formed one boundary and Aggipah Mountain (9929 feet) lay opposite. Completely arresting were the sheer cliffs beyond Ship Island Lake along which the outlet stream flowed. In the sun they formed a continuously vertical and sweeping wall. The near divide of the outlet creek was topped off with a series of slender and fragile gendarmes and pinnacles.

Clouds bore in ominously and there was thunder. We expected rain and turned back reluctantly. I lingered for a few last photos of the Clear Lake cirque. There was glory in this country, of harsh, timber line granite, out of which protruded those overpowering crags. There were a few trees and small meadows. But it was the lakes which gave the country charm and vitality. I would not have enjoyed it so completely but for their icy waters and connecting streams. Much of the country had not been explored except from the air. I yearned to go on down by Ship Island, under those terrible vertical walls and down Ship Island Creek to the Middle Fork of the Salmon River.

Our return trip to camp was an anticlimax. We chose to follow the trail instead of retracing our way across those fearsome snow slopes and the uneasy talus.

The rain did not materialize. We got hot under our rain gear as we ascended the nose of our piney ridge.

Beaver Slide Pass furnished a surprise. The contoured trail did not continue under the crags to connect with the pass. The

165

talus was too loose. Instead the trail descended sharply over bone-chilling rock to the center of the hollow. Here the trail angled back and forth, very steeply, through loose granitic soil. Snow had collected on this sunless north slope. The horses had churned it to water. And so as I moved upward, slowly, with heart pounding, I found myself plodding through a small rivulet of muddy snow water.

At the pass, Ernest wanted to follow the trail east along the Divide, for another four miles to camp. I pointed out that camp was just below us. I could see Welcome Lake and camp was in line with it. The trail was very steep. We descended the slope and in fifteen minutes were just above camp at the intersection with the Welcome Lake Trail.

17

L AST WEEKEND I went into a new realm of the wilds – this time, in Florida. Our immediate destination was the Sweetwater Springs in the Ocala National Forest about one hundred miles south of Jacksonville and in the center of the state. There we looked down upon a blue-green pool of water so clear it fairly jumped at us. It was flowing from under two limestone ledges in the bed of the pool and the movement of so much water gave the pool of shimmer and liveliness which was astounding. Its clarity was unbelievable. We could look through it to the sand and patches of wavy grass which covered its bottom. We could see uncounted numbers of fish hanging at various depths between surface and bed. Never in the natural world had I seen such clarity. Perhaps once at Oak Ridge in a de-ionized pool which shielded the swimming pool reactor, I had seen such water. But that water was still and lifeless and at the bottom was the fearsome Čerenkov glow from the reactor. Here was water of an inviting purity and clarity in a harmonious setting of live oaks and palmettos.

After lunch we drove to Juniper Springs some twelve miles above the cabin. From the Springs flowed a run of the same superlative clarity which joined the outflow of the Sweetwater Springs several miles below. Juniper Springs was walled in, was one hundred feet across, had the same blue-green sparkle of the Sweetwater Springs, and was enormously deep. It was said to be thirty feet to the caverns in its swirling depths. Again we looked down upon fish, swimming or resting, unafraid in the deep transparency. The setting of this spring was more sophisticated. It was the center of more than a hundred acres of well-appointed camping and picnic grounds. There were trailers, a lodge, an undershot water wheel, a mill, and other structures. But at the center was the clear bubbling pool of this gigantic spring.

Three canoes were drawn up below the pool. We were to use them to negotiate the length of Juniper Run, through a world as excitingly different as the springs themselves. George James and I rode with Gene Kaufman, a native who was steeped with knowledge of the area, which he told proudly and entertainingly. I had expected to paddle but he said it was unnecessary. So I rode the front of the canoe, with my camera, through a world of abundant life sharply divergent in its lushness and vitality from the dry undernourished forests which surrounded it. This luxuriant world was strung out along a thread of water, buffered from the world of men by miles of scrubby forest.

We asked about the springs. It seems clear that they pour from limestone caverns which can not be too far beneath the

168

surface of this low-lying state. We asked whence so much water came. The flow was steady — immense. No one seemed to know. One of the rangers said the water had been analyzed and contained minerals which could have come only from the vicinity of Asheville, North Carolina — eight hundred miles and two states away. Did these minerals and the moisture account for the lush, varied forest through which we floated?

It was an unutterable experience. In the narrow, more twisting parts of the run, Gene used his paddle. Always we were afloat on this amazing water which acted like a window to the world below — grasses, turtles, fish, hyacinths, logs — and mirroring the overhanging cardinal flowers, palmettos, hollys, pines, and cypresses. There were ibises, kingfishers, fish hawks, and owls. Life was abundant. Occasionally the run would widen into a pool and Gene would lift his paddle. Then we seemed to float without weight or substance on a surface which was but a film suspended between the breath-taking depths into which we looked and the incredible reflections of the vegetation and sky above. We seemed to be weightless — suspended by some miracle between two worlds. We moved, but without sense of motion. Only our eyes told us that there was drift as we slid over the depths. We hung dizzily and in silence without support, clinging, it seemed, to sheer transparency. We looked down into stark reflections of the sky, even as there were shadowy manifestations of an overlapping world of fish and wildlife and water plants. Never have I had such an experience — movement without motion, gliding without support, resting without weight. That lucent water, that placid mirror erased all normal sensation. In quietness, without feeling or stir, we drifted like spirits between heaven and earth. It was a dizzying experience — like weightlessness (not in a spinning cell in outer space) but in a world of color, and life, and delicacy, and inordinate beauty.

Most of the time the water had a vibrant blue-green clarity. It was like a filter which added richness and unwonted color to the reflections. But occasionally a small rivulet would enter from a bog and for a time there was a slight brownish cast to the run. Almost before we could note this, it would be clear again performing its feats of magic upon the overlying world. Sawgrass sometimes ripped at the canoe out of the depths of the stream. Pale hyacinths clung close. Yellow lilies bobbed with the current. Spikes of the rich cardinal flower rose from every swale. Palmettos overhung the run, their leaves like clusters of just-exploded rockets. Cypress knees were driven like stakes in every bog, the singular crowns of these trees spreading like green mist above us and always hung with airy, gray skeins of moss. This was a separate world, its parts drawn together by this mystic thread of water, clinging to the stream like beads to their string. The arid forest pressed close all along its course, sometimes creeping down almost to the water's edge. At other times the spreading swale pushed it back. Kingfishers plied the air above. And ibises rose awkwardly from their perches only to sail over us with matchless grace.

It was the place also of alligators, owls, raccoons, and turtles and moccasins − hardly any of which we saw − all drawn by the abundant life which gravitated to this transparent stream.

It was over all too soon. There were moments when the run spread into an expansive prairie that reminded me of the Okefinokee Swamp. Always there was that wondrous, limpid surface, reflecting the sky and trees above and revealing the fish and aquatic life beneath. It had a dual quality new to me. As old as America, perhaps it was one of these astounding springs which was Ponce de Leon's Fountain of Youth. The stream multiplied sensations, even as it neutralized others — a stirring, tantalizing world which touched everything with unimaginable alchemy.

That night a full moon glowed over Sweetwater Cabin. The great owls hooted in the distance. The spring poured out its liquid stream. And spiders worked their webs of witchery between wide-set palm trees.

18

BIG HORN CRAGS
IDAHO
1961

F EW PERIODS in my life have matched the prolonged, relentless, and intense anxiety of the three days just past. It arose over the disappearance in the Big Horn Crags within the Idaho Primitive Area of a woman botanist named Anna.

The day started disarmingly enough. Brandy proposed a hike from the site of our camp, which was about a half mile below Welcome Lake. A great bulging formation of granite came down to the very cook tent. It was an offshoot of the ridge which protruded from a higher divide and separated our camp from Welcome Lake.

We started up this pebble-faced granite and ascended it to the dividing ridge. As its slopes became more precipitous we angled off into the timber on the west face. Here there were scattered grass, loose talus, small bluffs, and sparse stands of timber. It was not easy going but it was not hazardous and we

172

made progress both laterally and vertically with infrequent rests. Eventually we intercepted the trail from Welcome Lake a few hundred feet from the top of the divide.

The divide at that spot was broad, level, and gritty, and broken by a scattered stand of pine. The elevation was around nine thousand feet. We eased off its south face into the timber and began to catch glimpses of a remarkable collection of lakes in the basin below. This was the Puddin Lake basin — a very wild area, untrailed, and hemmed in by savagely ragged mountains. There were a few meadows. By a quiet approach we hoped to see elk and other game. We proceeded as quietly as nine people could proceed and examined the area with some frequency with field glasses. Below us was forest, small meadows and emerald lakes. We finally counted a total of nine lakes, the most entrancing of which was one of considerable size, and the highest in the basin. It was far to the west of us and seemed to offer the most in beauty of surroundings and in remoteness. Edging slowly off the ridge, we moved in the general direction of this unnamed lake.

Four of the party grew impatient and dropped steeply into the basin. The other five of us held up for fear of dashing rocks on those who had gone on. Eventually we followed, but less precipitately, working through a bench of lodgepole pines to one of the meadows.

We were all very thirsty and found a string of slowly running pools from which we drank. Moving on another hundred yards, we found in a deep groin a freely running rivulet of very cold water coursing down flower-lined banks. We stopped and drank again. We were now at the lower edge of a shallow timbered ridge which we had glimpsed from above. Brandy thought if we got on its back we could follow it through the timber to the northwest and reach a point just above our unnamed lake.

As we started to arise, Anna demurred, saying she needed to rest. So we settled down again in moss along the banks of a freely running rivulet and enjoyed this very wild spot. Some, including Anna, ate a little, but I jokingly said the day was not over and I was saving my sandwich for an emergency. After perhaps twenty minutes we moved on through the covering woods. We reached the rounded back of the ridge and after a half hour found ourselves in sight of the green-black waters of our nameless lake. It lay so high, it was perhaps no more than fifty feet below the forested ridge crest we had been following. On our side there was a small beach, and a huge tree which had fallen parallel with the shore and slightly into the water.

There was a fringe of trees around the entire lake from which protruded rocky bluffs and above which were the stark chalky-gray angles of high above-timber line ridges. It was untrailed, remote. The lake lay open to the sky in a vast maze of intersecting ridges. It was a wild and beautiful lake.

Above the forest on the north and west were gray-fractured, angular faces of cliffs. Again I had reached a spot completely given over to wild game and seldom visited. The ruff of trees and beach, the rays of grass and flowering draws stretching up from the shore did not dilute my feeling. All around were gaunt pyramids of broken rock pushing above the forest into the domain of the thunderbolts. And back of us was the wide basin laced only with game ways. This was indeed wilderness – perhaps the wildest place I had ever been – and a part of the great Idaho wilderness.

In this grimly beautiful setting, we were soon to be chilled by fear for the safety of one who was then close by.

174

In the next half hour some went swimming in those frigid waters. Some soaked their feet. Some ate the balance of their lunches and some succumbed upon the soft moss for a noonday snooze. We looked at the ridges around us and saw a deep pass to the north of the lake. It was agreed that we would try to leave the area by that pass, and circling perhaps find another pass into Welcome Lake. Anna, eating her lunch fifty feet or so from the main crowd, may or may not have heard this decision. Shortly she moved north along the lake shore and took a place on a rock — in full view near the water and at the foot of a flowering draw. There, although a hundred yards away, she could be seen by the other eight. Ross Bennett had also left the party and was resting at the edge of the lake about half way between Anna and the rest of us.

I decided to take some photos from a bluff on the far side of the lake. I went north, stepping over Bennett where he rested. At the foot of the draw I asked Anna the name of the bright yellow flowers which were growing there.

"Arnica," she said.

Then probably motioning (although I don't recall for sure), I said,

"We are going out by that pass."

She replied, "I thought you would do that."

I then went sixty feet or so up the draw and took a couple of pictures. Descending I repassed her, where she had a scientist's hardbacked notebook on her knees making notes. I went along the shore flushing frogs into the water, where I could see them swimming with their short forelegs close to their bodies, propelled by the great scissor-strokes of their hind legs. I knew Dr. Greaves and his son were not far behind and I almost stopped to show the frogs to Paul. But time was short and I decided to go on. The lake was only 250 yards across and I could still see everyone but needed binoculars to identify them. I called across to Brandy, who was resting.

When I reached the top of the bluff, no more than ten minutes had elapsed since I had passed Anna. I could see two figures at her post and assumed that one of the fellows had stopped to talk to her. I then walked back along the shore to the main draw below the pass.

Thinking I would be the first at the pass, I climbed slowly taking photos and observing the birds and flowers. As I was nearing the top, I was surprised to see two figures and realized Doc and Paul had preceded me. Clouds and rain were gathering to the south among the crags across the lake and there was a sharp flash or two of lightning. Paul and Doc descended toward me to get out of lightning range, but we soon climbed again to the pass where we had agreed to rendezvous. It was a grim and bleak prospect to the north. Everywhere I looked were harsh, angular contours of nothing but rock.

I took the glasses and studied the frightening slopes of a pass into the Welcome Lake area. I wondered if we could drag our party up to it. There were too many bare, vertical bluffs to please me. The only hope lay in a fuzz of timber between which rock slides had torn ghastly perpendicular paths. Even if we could climb this slope, could we descend on the far side? Again a few straggling trees seemed to offer some hope. But it was not a certainty and I wished the others would come so we could get at it in daylight.

I whiled the time until Brandy should arrive, and when he did come Anna was missing. It did not alarm me but it was annoying. We were already late. Several went back to call her. Their shouts and rolling echoes were unanswered. The situation took on a serious aspect. If she could not hear, where was she? Had she fallen in that apron of giant boulders above the flowering draw where she had been sitting? There is nothing more potent, nor agonizingly eloquent, than silence in an area as cruel as this. She could be anywhere – unnoticed in those terrifying piles of rocks.

She did not come. Things were becoming serious. We abandoned our plan to circle back to Welcome Lake, and resolved to sweep that tilted boulder field above the flowers. There was hazard in this. The slopes were barely in repose and we stumbled across fragments of cliff which rocked under our weight. We had to spread far to protect those on the slopes below. It was hard tense work, and as the elastic string of our search drew into a knot in the draw, there was no sign of Anna. There was no inert form twisted among the car-size boulders – no answering cry to our anxious shouts – nothing.

That she had disappeared was incredible. She had been in sight of everyone. I had spoken to her, and yet she had vanished in the short ten minutes from the time I had repassed her until Ross Bennett and Tom Leggat had sat in the sun at the very spot where I had spoken to her. Had she ranged up the boulders and fallen? Had she followed a screen of trees to reach the pass ahead of the Greaveses and gone on down the bleak gorge beyond? Had she crossed under the bluff above her resting spot and fallen down the cliffs to the east? Had she reascended the shallow forested rim by which we had reached the lake and was even then making her way through the meadows and forest toward camp?

By a kind of consensus we decided she had gone back by the way we had arrived. But there remained that gnawing uncertainty. We swept the cliffs back of us with the glasses and

177

spread out through the woods before we reached the meadows, peering and looking, straining our eyes at the gloomy shadows in the woods for the secret they might hide. As we gained the open woods above the meadows, Brandy thought he found the track of a woman heading in our direction. He felt sure it was Anna's track and we were relieved. We had only to verify this when we reached camp. Our anxiety was dulled for the time.

As we slanted up the ridge, we intercepted a steep trail, which by short switchbacks went almost straight up. It was an elk trail and we followed it, clawing and slipping in the churned earth and gravel. On top we found ourselves only a few hundred feet west of the cairn marking the Welcome Lake trail. We hustled down this trail and walked into camp about 6:30 and received the numbing news that Anna had not returned.

It is hard to describe the effect. There was an amalgam of misgivings, forebodings, bewilderment, and incredulity. How could she have vanished with people all around her? What had happened to her; what was her condition?

The camp was galvanized. Amidst half-swallowed suppers, maps were drawn, plans laid, flashlights and extra batteries assembled, horses saddled, revolvers buckled on, rescue routes discussed and searching assignments made.

Three packers and Doc and Brandy were to ride as far as they could, hitch the horses, and descend again into the Puddin Lake basin and search it by flashlight. Two of the fellows were to go down Wilson Creek to a point commanding the ascent ridge and divide and build a signal fire in case she should return that way. Jim Moles, one of the packers, and I were to go up by the ascent of the morning, build another fire by which we hoped to guide her in.

We started out in deep dusk. I was tired from heavy exertions during the day. I knew in that thin air I would be no match for Jim. But we pushed on in half moonlight, never using our torches. We called continually and reached a point far higher on the ridge than we had made that morning.

We came to a pocket in a great balding face of the cliff. There were dead trees all around and a few fifteen-foot seedling firs. The site of our fire was a rocky niche overlooking Welcome Lake. I gathered squaw wood, Jim made shavings, and soon our signal fire roared up in the darkness. Jim was restless and decided to climb higher. He went on in the moonlit darkness. I kept in touch with him by shouts. The ridge, he reported, was like the comb of a roof and he stopped where he could command the divide and built another signal fire.

For a time I was alone with the lower fire and with my worries and thoughts. Under different circumstances the scene about me would have been a fantasy of beauty. I was on an eyrie of rock in the center of a vast basin of crags and pyramids. Below was the sheen of a lake and the shadow of a forest. The moon was obscured from me, but it shone through great windows of clear sky onto the cliffs behind me, touching them with unearthly light. It was a world one almost never sees, halfway between the brightness of day and the obscurity of full dark. The half-light showed a world which had never existed for man. He is not gifted for seeing in the darkness. Who would climb those rugged cliffs at night to see something which couldn't be imagined? Who would brave the chill of such an exposed place? And yet because of Anna's disappearance, I was high on a crag at night amidst scenes of haunting and spectral beauty. The cliffs which dropped precipitously all around me, my own weariness and half-thoughts, contributed eerily to the experience.

Suddenly there was a flare-up in my fire and a crackling explosion of light. I hastened around the screen of firs. The fire had crept close to a seedling fir four feet high. It became too hot and flared into flame — a blazing torch from a living tree. I was sorry.

The clouds thickened. Lightning flickered around us — the crags and pyramids flashed into sight and then went black again. There was a patter of drops on the rocks; I drew my jacket closer about me. Then I heard a shout. Jim was making his way back to me. We talked in low voices. There were no signal fires on the divide. Below we could see a light at the camp and the other signal fire down Wilson Creek. In the void below us we could hear the bells on the tethered horses.

Then Jim remembered that in our anxiety the horses had not been fed or watered. I thought this over, and decided that no one would now be descending those cliffs alone. We had accomplished our purpose in giving her a guide fire in the early evening. We decided to return.

So greatly does one become accustomed to the darkness, we hardly needed our lights. Each feature has a different gradient and shading. A shadow would mark a fallen tree. Our boots gripped perfectly. My only fear was loose gravel. We got into camp about 11 p. m. And as we went to feed the horses, out of the vastness behind us, there came the undulating wail and barking of coyotes. The wilderness had taken over.

I went to my sleeping bag about 12:20 a.m. and dozed fitfully, to be awakened at 3:30 a.m. by the sound of horses. I counted them as they stomped by. There were six horses, but the silence of the riders was ominous. I slipped on my boots and trousers and jacket and found Brandy down in the meadow with the horses. On their trip they had tied the horses on the divide and had descended by foot into the basin. With their torches they had again found our lake, had searched the draws and copses up to the pass. No Anna answered their shouts, or came into the beams of their flashlights.

At dawn we discussed further search plans. Richie would go to the roadhead and give the alarm to the road crew. Brandy would go down Wilson Creek. I would lead Tom Leggat and Jack Sheridan back to the lake. Jim Moles and Ross would ascend the ridge again and search the divide east and west. John Bradford and his father would take a stand on the divide at the Welcome Lake trail and pass on any signals from our party. Three shots if we needed help; two if we found her and all was well.

Tom, Jack, and I made up an emergency pack with a blanket, a pillow slip for splints, a gun for signaling, a canteen, and jackets. We had matches and flashlights. Tom carried the pack all day.

The night-searching party had been unable to ride the horses up the switchbacks of the Welcome Lake trail. On those violent slopes, horses were almost useless and we walked the whole distance and did not have the care of the horses. On top we checked on our signals with John Bradford and hunted the descending elk trail, the head of which John would mark with cairns.

When we descended to a lake, it had a rough, ugly shore with a ten-foot drawdown. We had never seen it before. It began to rain and the rocks were slick. We didn't know where we were. Instead of going back to a known point, we decided to circle to the right. This was an act of faith. Dimly visible in a low, overcast of clouds, the lake seemed to drain through a low

181

rim into an unknown creek. Through holes in the clouds, we saw unfamiliar ridges. It was a bad moment. We went over several ridges, expecting every time to see *our* lake over its crest. But no. We were thoroughly confused.

Eventually we climbed a little meadow, caught a glimpse of dark water through a thinness in the trees. I said, "This is it."

It was our lake; its features had been so burned in my memory, I could never have been mistaken about it. But we were very high on bluffs opposite the spot where we had eaten the previous day. And we had to find a way down off those bluffs to the shore. This we were able to do, and I walked out on the prominence from which I had taken photographs less than twenty-four hours before.

We first combed the lake shore between the big draw and grassy draw, examining every copse of trees where she might have crept for warmth had she been injured. We then climbed the rocks beneath the big butte and looked east. Tom thought she might have fallen there, and we saved it for a going-over on our return. We then worked back and forth between the two draws toward the pass and ridge crest. We were in sight and call of each other. There was no possible place of concealment which we did not examine.

Eventually we worked into the pass — a spot as empty and bleak as our search had been. I descended the far side to the bench which had blocked our view to the north on the previous day. The ravine was empty. Back to the pass for lunch. We heard a whistle and saw a figure to the east, high on the loose pyramid of rocks. On a hunch, I called,

"Is that you, Jim?" and Jim Moles worked down the rocks and through scattered trees to us at the pass. His shoes were almost in shreds. He had come alone across the lonely reaches above timber line.

While the others ate, I again descended from the pass to the north. I found a rudimentary trail made by game. There was nothing else. No signs. I wondered if any man had ever been there before. I went on down (dreading the climb on my return) until I could see a tiny empty meadow at the bottom and the violent, vertical cliffs guarding the pass. They were perpendicular – no ledges, no benches. After I had toiled back to the pass I cautioned Jim not to risk those crumbling cliffs, and he agreed, saying he would go to the foot of the ravine first. When we last saw him he was plunging down the rocks – his legs slightly bowed, the only living creature in sweeping Vs of talus which converged upon him from all sides. He had no pack or supplies. Audacious, fearless, conscientious, and tireless, he was one of the roughest, toughest, and most admirable persons I have ever known.

We again ran our three-toothed comb over the boulder field beneath the big butte. Jack wanted to examine the rim above the lake. Tom and I crossed the divide and searched the benches and troughs to its base. We called Anna's name at intervals. We heard nothing but worthless echoes. We met at the base. I felt somewhat encouraged that we had not found her injured, or any sign of her. She had surely, I thought, become separated from the party while she was still well. There was no sign of camera, pack, notebook, or discarded garments. I was sure she had not crossed the pass where we had just left Jim Moles. Tom felt she must have descended into the lower part of the main Puddin Lakes basin.

This made sense, as we were to learn later. Jim Moles eliminated the violent country to the north of the pass. Tom and I debated going down to the Puddin Lakes basin that afternoon, but we had promised to be back at camp by dark and to delay would add to the anxieties of those who remained.

As we were crossing the meadows, a helicopter came over the pass to the west, banked steeply and came to rest near us. The pilot had been instructed to pick up one of our party and search for an hour before dark. He was in a hurry — an overcast was coming in. Tom Leggat went with him in that open bubble which had stretchers for running boards. It swept back and forth a time or two, dashed toward the ground and then mounted upward and disappeared over the pass to the west.

At camp there was nothing to report. After supper Brandy announced plans to evacuate the party the next day by way of the Crags campground. We climbed a bluff above camp with a Forest Service walkie-talkie and sent messages to Brandy's father, to the Chamber of Commerce at Salmon for transport, and requested helicopters and searchers and ordered supplies for those who were staying.

We spent the last night around the campfire, taking the statements of those who had been on the hike with Anna or who had taken part in the search. I was to go out to help coordinate matters with the Forest Service.

I was impressed the next morning with the genuine concern of those in the party, people who had been thrown quite by chance with Anna and this impending tragedy. It was a sort of Cragland *Bridge of San Luis Rey.* They were generous in offers of field glasses, flashlights, and other equipment. People became individuals again out in that big country!

Our ride out was without incident. There were a few complaints about the speed with which we rode and about the dust. But Jim Moles and I were thinking of the lost woman and pushed the pace. I had Abby — a very fast horse which could keep the pace at a walk. At a few places where there was a stretch of downhill, the slower horses burst into a gallop and there was some consternation on the part of the riders.

At the roadhead we were met by folks from Salmon, and there began the long ride back in a microbus — five adults and three boys. Twice we had to get out and walk, and once we had to push the bus to get it started. I stopped at the Cobalt Ranger Station. No news, but I did get in touch with the office in Salmon and asked that Brandy senior meet me there.

At Salmon I went straight to the Forest Service office where I met Joe Denny, the dispatcher. For him I made a hasty map outlining the geography of our camp, the hike, the disappearance, and the searches that had been made and we related my data to Forest Service aerial photos.

Reports were coming in. The sheriff who had flown in that morning (Thursday) had been working the ground, but he had not been heard from. Tommy Farr, the ranger who was in the helicopter, complained that the dense forest in the Puddin Lakes basin interfered with visual observation. Joe Denny said that when a person is lost he usually spends the first day trying to get back to camp, and doesn't begin to help himself until the second day. He thought if Anna were not injured she would work down toward Wilson Creek. Dr. Greaves thought she had had a heart attack. I was reasonably certain she was somewhere in the basin and this view was shared by Tom Leggat. I mention these things to recall not only the hard facts, but the imponderables with which we had to deal.

Brandy senior, Joe Denny, and I went for a visit with Anna's sister, who by a coincidence lived in Salmon. We then went on up to see Gene Powers, Supervisor of the Salmon National Forest, who was in bed with dizziness and nausea as a

185

result of overexertion with one of the forest fires in that region. We all talked at some length but it was obvious we were at the end of our rope and must call on the great facilities of the Forest Service.

We were faced also with hellish uncertainties. Suppose she should not be found, either alive or dead, for how long should we press the search? That was a bottomless pit — a kind of circumstantial quicksand.

The following day, when Floyd Iverson, the Regional Forester in Ogden, gave instructions for the Forest Service to do all that it could with its own forces, the men sprang into activity. There was a great bustle as packs and supplies were assembled for the search crews, along with brawny outdoorsmen who were bursting with vitality.

Brandy senior had to get some new boots for young Brandy, who had walked the feet out of his old boots. Brandy senior and I came back to Denny's office about 11 a.m. We were sitting on the floor indulging in desultory conversation with Denny and his assistant, when the radio squawked and there came over it the electrifying words:

"Lost woman found; lost woman found. In good condition; in good condition."

All the tenseness of the past seventy hours drained away.

There was of course much to be done — recalling the search parties; relaying the word to Anna's sister; getting word to young Brandy; talking to Gene Powers — thus disassembling the web of communication and activity which had built up so rapidly around the disappearance. But the sense of relief and relaxation was massive and deep-felt. It was not until late afternoon when we had a scheduled radio contact with Brandy that he heard of the rescue. This spread of several hours between our receiving the news and passing it on to him, even with all the modern gadgets available to us, reflects the ruggedness of the area involved.

Although the details are not clear, Anna on the day she became separated from the party had climbed from her place by the lake to the rendezvous pass. Apparently she arrived there at the precise moment that Doc Greaves and his son had vacated it because of the storm. She decided she had missed the party and determined to return by our route in. How she missed intercepting the five of our party who were then ascending to the pass is the prime mystery. She returned by the Puddin Lakes basin, missed the turn off over the ridge to camp and proceeded on down the drainage to Wilson Creek along the banks of which she was spotted from the air three days later.

A few more comments are pertinent. As I consider those days, I think how precious in such an environment and under such circumstances is one human life. All the terrific complex of experience, knowledge, intelligence, and aspiration which inheres in a human life we were determined to save (that is, if it were not already lost). In that massive, untrailed and jagged terrain, a single human was the focus of all thought, activity, and anxiety. Wilderness had become a place where a human being could be seen and valued as an individual.

It is one of our problems today that our huge cities have become frightening colossi. The individual exists, for himself and a few who know him. Otherwise he is one of a mass to be thought of in the mass and shunted about in streams of traffic, in streams of thought, and in easy academic classifications. It took this wilderness experience to etch again the importance of a single person.

19

MURIE RANCH
JACKSON HOLE
WYOMING
BADLANDS
SOUTH DAKOTA
NORTH DAKOTA
GLACIER NATIONAL PARK
BISON RANGE
MONTANA
ELBO RANCH
JACKSON HOLE
SHEEP MOUNTAIN
WYOMING
1962

E VERYWHERE we went on our trip this summer we were
met by extremes and novelties in weather: 104° (very
unusual) at Badlands National Monument in South Dakota; a
thunderstorm and prolonged drenching rain at the Theodore
Roosevelt National Memorial Park in North Dakota; rain, snow,
and premature cold at Medicine Grizzly Lake in Glacier Park;
more rain at Red Eagle Lake; uncommonly slick roads out of
Red Eagle Creek; rain at Swiftcurrent Campground with new
snow on Grinnell Glacier; extraordinary clouds over the Teton
Mountains; an onset of snow in Jackson Hole, and a bitterly
cold ride up Granite Creek; and finally here at home a
monumental overnight rain after a month of drought.

On our trip, we enjoyed with Olaus and Mardy Murie in
Wyoming the best of man's world and of the natural world.

Theirs is a home with books and paintings, and beautiful carvings and rugs. There was also humility, and sensitivity and a cherishing of the world of nature. There we had wood fires. There was no lawn. The sagebrush and gophers and plants of the desert and forest crept up to the house. Bears came and looked in the windows, as did western jays. The calls of the owls and coyotes were subjects of daily conversation. At the Muries', no one was ever bored with the great outside world. One afternoon we saw dark shapes emerging from the woods, primordial beasts who moved freely in and out of the Murie sanctuary — a cow moose with two calves. She moved leisurely, stopped and looked at us as though *we*, like she, were a part of the natural world. The calves, unawed, butted their mother and nursed before our eyes. This home was an oasis of civilization but one which had subordinated itself to the natural world about it. And people come there from over the world to sense the essential nobility and humbleness of that home.

Olaus was convalescing from a drastic operation. His body was wasted and his color ashen. Sometimes he had an inward look as though he were concerned with another world not too far away in time. But then he would smile, and make a trenchant observation in a strong voice. On his walk a quarter of a mile or so to the lily ponds, one realized he was still immersed in the natural world. A colorful geranium leaf or the ripe puffiness of the goat plant took his attention. He wondered about the moose and ravens and why there were fewer moose this year. He smiled at the grace and lightness of the jays, as they swooped in, lit on his hand, and took a piece of bread. He discussed the owls which called to each other the night before, and there was gentle argument whether the male had the high note or was responsible for the deeper booming hoots. Olaus had had many honors from the world of men, but he bore them lightly. He constantly heeded the vast natural world about him — the world of insects, of plants, and of animals. He brooded over the precarious balance by which man has so far maintained a place in this world. And he wondered if man's niche is as secure as is generally thought. He was concerned about mass insect controls and the disturbance of natural controls. In him we observed a highly civilized being who was alarmed and uneasy at what man is doing. He felt safer and more at home in that great other-world and was perplexed and disturbed by the extremes to which man goes in his ignorance. Man seeks to eradicate a single enemy with clouds of poisonous dust which, like blind justice, destroys friends as well. While he and Adolph, his brother, sought to learn more about the infinitely complex natural world, other men in their ignorance were slowly destroying this very world which sustains them.

Mardy Murie said it would be so easy in that divine place to ignore the problems of men and all the excesses that are being committed. But both were avid readers; both had a loyalty to race and species; and both wanted to know. Each staunchly believed in human freedom. Each believed that in the right to inquire and learn lies the salvation and the survival of mankind. One becomes fortified in his own beliefs at this oasis of culture in its setting of the primeval.

It seemed tragic that Olaus's powerful and inquiring mind which has so much to contribute to both worlds may succumb far too soon to the ravages of a disease which no man understands. He was fighting to finish a book, to do more paintings, to bring further order into the studies he has been making over half a century. Here was man at his best, beleaguered by weakness and disease but unafraid. He had savored deeply of life and found it good, and we came away uplifted.

BADLANDS OF SOUTH DAKOTA

As usual on our trips to wild country we had tremendous experiences. At the Badlands of South Dakota we saw the break between a high grassy prairie and a much lower plain. Between these two levels were the sharp, fantastic pinnacled breaks known ás the Badlands. The beginning of the degradation from good grass country was unbelievably clean. The line of the break wavered in direction but it was always unmistakable. Sometimes a chunk of grassland would slip down a few feet, intact. But most of the time the discontinuity between grass and the harsh, barren disorder was acute. The earth involved is sedimentary in origin. It maintains itself in a glaring frieze of spikes and cones and deeply angled gullies over long periods with minimal disintegration, because of the paucity of rainfall.

I overheard a man say there had to be some ingredient in the clay which held it stiff. It is a hard, starchy material which crumbles underfoot. It gleams in the merciless sun and is carved in fantastic shapes with an appearance of solidity. There were windows and sharp towers and battlements. In places the run-off of water from infrequent cloudbursts was through tunnels worn through the clay. It is one of the richest places for fossils in the country.

We wanted the feel of this desert fantasy. Such heat I had seldom experienced. At the campground down on the lower plain, below the gleaming, bizarre, three-dimensional escarpment, the heat had a solid malevolence, heightened by a ceaseless wind. In some parts of the world a breeze is cooling.

191

Here it was like the blast of a furnace enveloping the body in waves from which there was no escape. One wanted to come up for air. But when one took a deep breath, he gulped air several degrees warmer than his body temperature. Curious, slatted shelters which made us think of prairie schooners arched over the tables provided by the Park Service. In photos they had seemed grotesque creations which detracted from the fine, scenic desert. Actually, they proved to be havens from the glare and heat, from the shelter of which we could better view this dazzling world. Children clambered all over a knife-edged pinnacle, which rose a hundred feet above the edge of the campground. I followed some of the paths on the disintegrating clay. The pyramid would have softened and flowed away in a rain such as we are having here in Tennessee today. But in that dry clime, it broke apart physically in chunks a half inch or so in cubic content, which rolled under my feet on the slopes. But the clay broke only under mechanical pressure, and the sharp wedge which looked down on the camp and over which the youngsters clambered seemed to be held together by invisible forces. It was like potter's clay which had been through the first firing. It was brittle and unglazed and rattled apart as people clambered over it. But the pinnacles and spines which broke the skyline to the north could not be climbed, and yielded only to the scanty rains and winter freezes. The scene had a curious timelessness — this clay with little underlying rock to sustain it.

Relief from the heat came at sunset. The white glare turned to gold and then to copper, as the sun sank behind a sharply-honed ridge. A leaden cloud from which lightning flickered swept in from the south — and there was a hint of rain as well as of coolness in the air. But the rain never came, even as the coolness remained, and the façade of cliffs to the north gleamed oddly in the silver radiance of the moon.

BADLANDS of NORTH DAKOTA

From the Badlands of South Dakota we drove to the Badlands of North Dakota. Between the two there was a pleasant interlude through the forests and low meadows of the Black Hills — then through grassy wastes and the occasional gold and black bands of the strip farms. We stopped at the southernmost of the three Theodore Roosevelt Memorial Parks.

This was a different kind of bad land. It was as deeply incised, but here the terrain was underlain with bands of rock and shale and lignite — instead of the homogenous structure of concreted clay to the south. There was some grass and sagebrush and a river — the Little Missouri. We wound through a deeply dissected plain to the pleasantly named campground — the Cottonwood Grove.

We arrived late and I pitched our tent carelessly. Clouds were collecting and streaming in from the north. There was lightning and quick bursts of thunder which I disdained. I had seen too many storms dissolve in midair out in this dry, western country. I would not be fooled again. We ate slowly while the wind and clouds came closer, and I began to question not only my judgment but the toughness of those brittle cottonwoods. And then the burst of rain! It sheeted in and gathered in a little drain at the head of our tent. I tried scratching little ditches into the ground hoping to divert it from our tent site.

At dark there was a letup. We crawled into our tent where we shucked off our wet clothes and crept into muggy sleeping bags. During the night the rain was intermittent. Our tent was wet inside and out. In the damp interlude, just before dawn we heard the measured notes of a great owl – precise and non-earthly. The calls seemed to mark the unhurried pulse of our surroundings.

We arose in the damp, built a fire, and had a damp breakfast. We packed quickly, trying to get as much as possible under cover without added moisture. But our sleeping bags were wet, as was the tent and the tarp underneath.

On the way out we stopped at Park Headquarters and were shown the cabin in which Theodore Roosevelt had lived eighty years ago. I have never been more impressed by a memorial to a man. In Roosevelt's day the rigor of the plains, and the blundering tools and equipment and structures of man had met there in a draw. The plains and the buffalo herds were still in retreat, but man had made only a few advances. He had not conquered. He had harmed the wilderness but not beyond recovery. And my mind quickened as I looked at this vivid restoration of a day long gone. I felt that the dedicated men in the Park Service had made time stand still for me and for a few moments I merged myself with this past.

The scene changed. Two afternoons later in the breezy dryness of a perfect day we hung out our things to dry at the campground along the beautiful and clear Belly River in Canada's Waterton Lakes National Park. Across from our low bluff was an immense yellow plain, backed by mountains. The yellow plain was a part of an Indian in-holding.

GLACIER NATIONAL PARK

The following night we spent with the Ed Hummels (Superintendent of Glacier National Park). He said that the

194

Sierra Club was having one of its "high-light" trips in the Park and he thought he knew where they were camped and that we could join them. This appealed to us. It would afford an opportunity to see some of the back country. Our stuff was carried in by horse. We walked.

The Sierra Club folks were camped at the upper end of Medicine Grizzly Lake, and had numerous and sundry tents scattered about. Two large tarps provided additional shelter. Some of the party, including the Wayburns (Ed was president of the Sierra Club), were out climbing the massive wall at the head of the lake. On the cliffs hung a plunging cascade fifteen hundred feet high.

We picked the top of a low moraine for our tent site. The clouds were black and I had no intention of pitching our tent in another drain. By now we had learned to pitch quickly. Even so, we were caught by the rain. We rigged the nylon fly across the tent. It worked beautifully. It could be tautly drawn and provided shelter on each side of the tent for our duffle bags. But the sagebrush and vegetation were high between our tent and the cooking fire and our legs were soaked as we sloshed back and forth. Rain whipped in with the wind, and cooking became a battle between the fire and the damp. And because of the weather there was some concern for the safety of those who had climbed high.

Anne and I were not adequately dressed for the combination of rain and wind which swept across the lake. There were two fires and I helped with the wood, but we were both strangers to the routine. We watched anxiously the great heights about us, and finally in the last stages of twilight spotted three figures. Soon we made out seven more carefully working their way down.

195

Anne laughed at the simplicity of eating in the rain. We used our Sierra cups for everything — soup, macaroni and cheese, gelatin salad, and coffee. These courses were being dished up under the tarp as those from the climb approached through the gloom.

In the whole party were two doctors and a fourth-year medical student. There were scientists and teachers — one family of six and another of five. Altogether they composed an interesting and cheerful group, which did not seem too disturbed by the weather.

It was now full dark, although a little light found its way into the cirque and reflected from the lake. People were bumbling shadows, sprayed with rain and buffeted by the wind. Occasionally a beam from a flashlight cut the darkness but that was all. Little Lori Wayburn was damp and chilled. Her straw hat was pulled far down over her face for warmth. I pulled her close to me and wrapped my jacket around her shoulders. She was shaking with the cold, as was I.

While I snuggled Lori a conference was taking place around the fire in the rain. All I could see was a ring of dark shapes, and the spiteful tongues of flame licking at them under the scourge of the wind. Eventually a spectral voice issued from the group. Everybody listened. Decision would be made in the morning whether camp would be moved the next day. It all turned on the weather. It was then eight o'clock. I said, "I am going to bed," and the scientist from California said, "That is the best suggestion I've heard."

Amenities were abridged. Even Anne forewent washing her teeth. We waded up through the sagebrush again getting drenched to our knees. We stumbled around in the dark taking off our boots amongst a maze of tent cords and guy ropes. We laid the boots flat under the fly. Inside the tent we removed our soaked outer clothes and bundled them at the foot of our sleeping bags. Then we flounced into our bags, flopped as we pulled the wrinkles out and sank gratefully to the hard flatness of our beds. It rained and blew all night, but we were snug and dry. The next morning we pushed aside the damp folds of the tent front and looked out. It was still blustering, and the ridges just above the camp were white with snow! Clouds blotted out the rim of the great cup in which we camped. The lake hugged the bottom and streams augmented by the rain slithered down the incredibly steep walls to feed it.

It was a grim scene. We were shut in by high mountains now slick with snow. Only at the mouth of the lake was there an outlet. It lay to the east and the V between the mountains was blotted out by clouds. I wondered if we would move. A warden was to meet Anne and me next day on the far side of the divide, and if we were tied down by weather we could not make our rendezvous.

These were my thoughts as people stumbled to the cooking area. The first thing was a fire and this we had. Then came red-haired Emily Weber — petite and dynamic. She was one of the cooks. Nothing daunted her — wind, rain, and bluster left her unperturbed. Breakfast began to take shape. As it did so, the clouds down the lake began to thin and the sun broke through and transformed the back wall into a vivid green.

"We are going to move," shouted the leader.

Move we did, but the sun did not fulfill its momentary promise. Clouds boiled back and the whole morning was a succession of fantastic glimpses through the mist of frightful slopes and of forbidding mountain walls. We were to go over the Triple Divide Pass between the upper reaches of Atlantic Creek upon which we were camped and Hudson Bay Creek on the north. The Pass had a heart-quickening appeal to me. It lay just a few hundred feet lower than the modest peak by the same name, which stood at the very top of the continent dealing out waters: on the northeast to the St. Mary River and ultimately to Hudson Bay; on the southeast to a tributary of the Milk River, to the Missouri and ultimately to the Atlantic Ocean at the Gulf of Mexico; and on the west to the Flathead, Clark Fork, and Columbia River and ultimately to the Pacific Ocean.

We had seen the low bump of Triple Divide Peak from St. Mary Lake two days before. I had yearned to go there. And here I was, two days later, camped at the foot and preparing to go through the Pass. I could hardly wait. Some of the hardier souls proposed to climb by the great slope directly to the north rather than by the trail. I joined them knowing that the experience of passing that monumental divide in the raging wind and snow of a premature winter would be induplicable. I was restless to down my breakfast, strike our tent, and set out.

We climbed slowly up ever-steepening slopes, through the rain-drenched sagebrush and the greasy crowns of bear grass. To cross this particular divide in snow and storm and the adversities of 7500 feet of altitude was terrific. The leader, Al Weber, moved steadily. Ten of us were strung out behind. I paused for pictures and strained to keep my place. Up to the first ledge — back and forth, going higher each time — Medicine Grizzly Lake flattened out in its great cup and the sun occasionally burnished the clouds to the east. Up and up, the vegetation thinned and so did the air.

Many things stirred me — that continental roof above me — the great glacial basin below — timber line — and my own limitations drawing out thinner and thinner. All these things

198

built up with the altitude to a kind of lifetime climax. I felt the altitude about the time we exceeded the height of Mt. LeConte in the Smokies (6593 feet).

The others drew away. The vegetation had given out. Our way was steep over a barren of timber line rock. Triple Divide Pass was shut in by mist and the wind began to sting my cheeks and my laboring lungs. All the dross of civilization was slipping away. I was alone, although I could still see above me the figures of the others nearing the Pass. The day had become pure struggle and expectation. How simple, how pure my desire − to get up there in the wind and cold and to stand on that spot in the snow.

The others waited at the Pass. Although I was not over ten minutes behind them, Al said he didn't want to leave anyone on the wrong side of the divide. It was one of the bleakest places I have been, and one of the most dramatic. Fog choked the Hudson Bay valley. Everything in sight was dusted with snow. There were two small lakes, half full of ice − black peaks almost too steep for snow, and at our feet, an inch and a half of new snow!

This was it! Just above us − somewhere on the tortured rock of the peak − was the top of the continent. A grim lonely barren, carrying its burden of geography. Little do we think of the high drama of these points from our comfortable vantages far down and far away on the continent. There was a little yellow in the rock and a touch of blue in the lakes. Otherwise, Triple Divide Pass flaunted its remoteness in broad sweeps of black and white. Above most life, above the continent − was the Triple Divide!

I loved the extremes of it and Al Weber consented to my remaining until Anne came up the trail. I was there, or just

199

below the crest in a recess under a rock, for an hour. My face stung with cold. I had on six layers of clothing, but by the time she arrived, I was shaking convulsively.

On the Hudson Bay, the trail took off through a waste of tumbled rock and of low, stunted timber line trees. It cut back through a rock bar and descended the first great step of a new cirque. At its foot we moved into young timber amongst wan, pastel shades of flowers scorched by the new snow. Deceptive threads of water cascaded down interminable slopes from hidden lakes and snow fields. They were deceptive in that they seemed a mere wisp of water. But when we came to them we had to pick our way carefully to cross.

On down through the woods the wind tore at us. There was no escaping it. It reached us wherever we were. Even among the big trees, we were aware of it as it raced through their tips. We went down and down.

Eventually we caught the leaders at Red Eagle Lake. We had leap-frogged the designated camping place because of the weather and were far down the valley in the shelter of the Douglas firs. They had a fire and boiling water and gratefully we drank scalding lemonade. But there was not too much we could do until the pack string came in with the food, utensils, and tents. We did drag in a lot of wood for the fires and waited.

We spent another rainy night at Red Eagle Lake and then Anne and I were met by the warden, and we skidded and slopped five more miles over a muddy trail to his truck. Ours was a wild experience in high altitudes in great forests, but also up where the mountains were bold blocks, and wedges, and pyramids. Only the lakes were oval, and the valleys, soft with the curves of glacial action. That night we camped again in the rain, on Swiftcurrent Creek in Glacier National Park.

200

As we started out for Grinnell Glacier we could see only a sliver of the glacier through curtains of mist. We moved through rich forests past two lakes and then began to ascend the valley wall. Below us was Grinnell Lake — a milky jade in color. We then angled up the green sidewall toward the head of the canyon. The headwall was broken by a waterfall, whose stream oozed out from under the black recesses of the glacier itself. On the ascent, we looked up side valleys, green and inviting under the mist, but hemmed in on each side and at the end by grim cubes and trigons and pyramids of mountains. Some slopes were flushed with red; some had great flowing strata of dirty gray rock; but all were beetling, vertical and precipitous. Indeed, except around the openness of the lakes, in the huge area that is Glacier Park almost everywhere we went, we had the impression of being shut in by bald and gigantic, snowy mountains.

The Grinnell Glacier covered half a square mile. A mountain wall rose above it, but it lay broad and open and unconfined. As we worked along the trail we had expansive views of it and of the figure of a man, fantastically small, moving along its edge. Then we were shut off by the gray drabness of a moraine. It was when we surmounted the moraine, that we felt the might of the glacier itself. It was close, although on a scale that was deceiving. Almost at our feet was a lake gray and opaque, like dirty dish water, in which great chunks of ice were floating. It was a dead, breathless place. There was not a ripple. Along its edge was a frightening waste of broken rocks of huge proportions — trackless and formless. Two or three small triangular flags seemed to mark a trail through the confusion, but in that barren jumble man had made little impression.

I left Anne on the moraine and went out across that chaos of rocks for a closer look at the glacier. I had no intention of going onto it alone, although two men had walked out on it and quickly became mere mites on its vastness. What I wanted to see was the line where glacier and the stony waste joined. There was no difficulty in defining the line of junction. The ice was dirty, full of grottos of small interlocking cones and scallops, black with rock dust, and dripping with the melt. The beginning of the moraine was not a sharp line. It was not a ridge, but was shallow in depth — a huge and confused blanket of stone and dust and boulders on a vast shelf of solid rock, almost as large as the glacier itself, which pitched downward toward the waterfall.

At the low center of the shelf, a stream of dirty water poured from under the glacier. It swirled down a channel which had been gouged and torn in the rocky shelf and ended in the waterfall we had seen on the ascent. In the tremendous cirque of the valley the waterfall had seemed a mere tangled thread. Here at its source I found a substantial stream, which was so wide I had difficulty in crossing it dry shod. I moved out across the horizontal ledge, past the blanketing detritus. From the lip, I could see a chain of lakes far down the valley — each progressively clearer, the farther it lay from the glacier.

The cliff edge was almost devoid of vegetation — a bare bedding of rock. Then came the vast, tormented covering of rock fragments, bisected by the silted stream. Then came the scalloped gloom of the glacier's edge; then, the broad rock-strewn expanse of the ice itself, slit with crevasses; and above that, the mighty encircling cliffs of Mt. Gould and the Garden Wall. On the north edge there was the tumbled moraine where Anne awaited me.

In that huge waste Anne lost sight of me almost

immediately. The three flags marked a way, but not a path. I was lost to view in the mazes of the rock fragments. I was never more alone. I was of no more significance or importance there, than a snow flea on an ice field. This was a place to visit but not to live. No vegetation, no animals, a harsh waste of raw rock and ice. Here man could learn humility, but could not live for long. The raw primal message was clear. The earth was born in violence, and violence still lurked at its edges. Man had adapted and made his home where things could grow. Up here, he came only to look and climb. Every expedition to such places anywhere in the world originated and, if lucky, terminated in gentler lands where man could thrive.

People have a huge curiosity about such places and in the course of the day we saw more than thirty persons who had elected to visit the glacier.

We spent another night at the Swiftcurrent campground, departing in the morning for the west side of the Park. We saw two mountain sheep — a tawny gray with magnificent curving horns. They crossed the road leisurely and ate their way up to a ledge which they nimbly climbed. They were the true natives, at home in the ruggedness, able to find food and survive the severities of weather and terrain.

Later from the road we saw two goats in a rugged milieu above the highway. One was grazing on a tilted bench. The other was forty or fifty feet above it, at rest and draped much like an old dish rag across a sharp rock — hind feet on one side, front feet on the other. It was looking down with mild interest at its companion. It was so at rest, so at home, I envied it the simplicities of its existence. It could live on the very fringes of the upper belt of vegetation. Nature clothed it. No middle men, no advertising, no soil banks. Here was living at its simple best. Its relationship to the land was artless and direct.

BISON RANGE

On the way south we stopped at the National Bison Range, a refuge of 19,000 acres. It is in the lower Flathead Valley, a great arid upland of grass with a scattering of forest. We first saw a herd of twenty-five buffalo in an earth groin, well below us. A second herd was likewise in a grassy ravine.

We saw one mule deer resting out of the sun in the shade of a ponderosa pine. A little later we heard a rattling in the dry vegetation. It was an antelope bounding headlong down a steep, grassy slope. From the higher slopes we looked across squared patches of cultivation in the Flathead Valley to the Mission Mountains.

Extensive as it was, the Bison Range was not wilderness. It had a fence around it to prevent movement out and to prevent movement in. It was acquired in 1908 by the American Bison Society to provide a refuge for the beleaguered buffalo. Its aim has been achieved. The herd is substantial and is thriving. But there is management. Each buffalo is inoculated. In the fall selected buffalo are driven into enclosures where they are fattened and the surplus is slaughtered. Water is impounded and pumped to troughs in some of the areas.

At headquarters there were some fenced enclosures where persons could see buffalo and elk at close hand. I realized this was a far cry from the enormous, thousand-mile migrations of the vast herds a hundred years ago. But those spectacles are gone forever. It was a boon, just to see the clumsy, primordial hulk of a buffalo in the flesh. I have commented elsewhere upon the massive shoulders and hump and the skinny hind legs and black, grizzly head which seemed to be pitched inches below the line of the back bone. The great coat of hair which produced the buffalo robes was, in the summer heat, coming off in broad flakes. The hind quarters and middle were bare. The pelt on the shoulders varied with individual animals. The great head, bushy with hair, and with eyes which seemed lost in their hairy surroundings, hung low to the ground. The hump was an enormous swelling above and around the shoulders and so unbalanced the animal it could not roll on its back. Indeed, one old bull rolled in a dusty place as we watched. He dropped to the ground, rolled on one side and, instead of turning over to the other side like a horse, raised his great bulk onto his fore feet and then lay down again in the dust to scrub the other side. Our young guide spoke of the unique bodies of the bison. He said they are so strong and massive in their shoulders and front quarters and so frail in the rear, that they actually pull themselves up over steep places with their front feet − using their rear legs as braces for the body as it gathers itself for another lunge. One cow had two calves and, as they nudged and butted her for her milk, there was no doubt that even this strange species was a member of the family of mammals.

JACKSON HOLE

We spent seven nights at Elbo Ranch on the east side of Jackson Hole. On the second night and every night thereafter, we heard the sharp, quick, pulsating bark of a coyote, strung like vanishing puffs of air on a thin, long drawn-out wail. It is the wildest sound I know. It had excitement and vitality and mystery — and produced a lingering nostalgia for days that are gone. We listened, alert for the high thin wail, rent and split by the pulsing bark, like bursts of water from a fountain. Often it was far away, like a barely heard echo. One morning it was close by. Anne dashed out and saw the coyote himself standing not two hundred feet away.

A half hour later she and Bob Cooney and I, with our field glasses, went coyote hunting. I went casually, skeptically, expecting to see nothing but the glory of the dawn on the Tetons across the valley. This we saw too — but we had hardly started when Bob stepped back and said, "There it is."

And there it was, even for me to see — long-haired, sharp-faced, alert ears — gray, with a tinge of brown and lightness around the face — standing casually but with an electric alertness in the edge of the sagebrush. Sometimes only its head showed. But it was close enough for us to see — its eyes slanting upward like slits across its cheeks. There was tenseness and alertness, and something wistful in those eyes. Here was the desert hunter engrossed in its way of life — the only life it knew. But there was nothing vicious or heavy in the fine angular lines of its head. Once we saw it sitting, for several minutes, facing the sun. Then it departed trotting away from us with purpose.

"He still has hunting on his mind," said Bob.

SHEEP MOUNTAIN

I visited Sheep Mountain again. Anne and I hiked there with Olaus and Mardy Murie on our first visit to Jackson Hole in 1948. On that trip we backpacked and briefly lost our way in hellishly unstable country at a very high elevation. As I rode up on horseback this time, the mountain and the high bosom of grassland by which we had approached the top was exactly as I had remembered it.

On this year's trip, our party worked up from a different direction following a ridge through trees. Here and there was an occasional opening with an avenue of tawny grass. I foresaw that we would emerge out of the trees onto that same high, grassy, rounded meadow. The meadow bulged above us, and beyond and above it was a narrow crescent of snow and broken rock. There was talk of going back. But I said,

"No, there's the top, not more than a mile away." And I started on – walking.

It was important to get there. Sheep Mountain was no longer just the summer abode of wild sheep; it had become the highest point, and anchoring corner, of a proposed new wilderness area. It was imperative that some of us get there and take our Forest Service companion with us.

I walked slowly in the soft grass. Sheep Mountain was over 11,000 feet high – 3000 feet higher than Anne and I had recently climbed in Glacier Park. But at my slow pace I ascended easily. After awhile the others followed on horses. This was a gallant sight – the horsemen, deployed across the reaches of the meadow, coming toward me. Beyond and far below them, were the outlines of all of Jackson Hole. And beyond it, and standing like a wall, without depth or body were the misty serrations of the Tetons.

Some of the horsemen passed me. The wind tore at us and several chased their hats, which were swept from their heads and bounded like tumble weeds across the turf. I was a dude and I had read down at the ranch: "Be sure and secure your hats." This I had done with a piece of cord tied across the top of my hat and under my chin. Bob Casebeer of the Forest Service disdained using some of my cord, and lost his hat over the edge of the abyss.

Bob Cooney left his horse with the others, and he and I made the final pyramid together. He thought it was at least seven hundred feet high as we looked at one of its sheer sides from the last tongue of meadow. The wind pounded at us in solid gusts and as we started up we kept well away from the vertical north slope. I was fearful of the wind and also of that highly fractured rock. I didn't want to be blown over the cliff nor did I want it to disintegrate beneath me. Bob found a trace of a path and we picked our way over the razor-edged stones. Once I saw the brilliant indigo blue of the creeping forget-me-not. But mostly there was little vegetation, just a heaped jumble of stones covering the stratifications of limestone which gave shape to the pyramid. Our sharp ascent gave us an eagle's view of the horse party. It was huddled on a shelf behind a break in the meadow. Two hikers had detached themselves from the group. How tiny were their figures as they moved along the rim toward us. One proved to be Bob Casebeer, now hatless. When he caught up to us later, he was ruddy from the wind. The other was George Marshall.

In the thin air, I had to rest for short periods and Bob Cooney pulled away from me. Then he would stop for a look and I would catch him. Two or three times in especially sharp gusts of wind I caught his arm to hold my balance. But we made excellent time and it was only an hour to the top from our lunch place whence I had started walking. At the top our first look was down the cliff edge to a U-shaped valley with a small lake and some timber. This valley opened out into the main Gros Ventre far below. Then we looked to the east, to a broad expanse of tan-gray mesas reaching illimitable distances to the horizon, the edges of which broke away into formidable cliffs. Occasionally the mesas swelled to a snow-spotted peak similar to the one we were on. There were no trees — just rock and peaks and a bit of snow and these sweeping, smooth, thin-grassed mesas. It was marvelously inviting. One had the feeling he could hike on with easy command across those smooth surfaces for days. They were much like the meadow we had ascended. But like it, they were interrupted and broken by cliffs, and down-sweeping talus slopes.

Bob Casebeer and George reached the top after a time and we got out maps and a compass, and discussed boundaries for this wilderness of wildernesses. It was good to be up there with those three wonderful guys.

That morning, we had started out in hard, bright sunshine. But as the day wore on, clouds and murkiness took over. After returning to the horses, we descended in cool windy gloom. The weather was changing. In the night we heard the rattle of rain on the roof of the lodge. And when we arose, we looked out upon an inch and a half of snow!

20

ALASKA

1963

THE COMPARATIVE deliberateness of driving to Alaska, as compared with flying, seemed to me to offer a proper conditioner of the mind and spirit for a visit to this vast frontier land.

I am convinced that the prolonged and sometimes rocky build-up of the road trip contributed to our acute enjoyment of the whole experience. There was dust and mud and a rough surface for over a thousand miles. The very word "thousand" had a kind of magic connotation. Travel was considerably easier than that experienced by Alexander Mackenzie in 1789, but considerably worse than by modern interstate.

The very distance was a kind of hurdle. I remember how the onset of the unpaved portion was postponed. The first milepost was at Dawson Creek, British Columbia, but there was a reprieve of a hundred miles. After we passed Fort St. John, there it was — the dirt and rocks all cobbly and rough. With memories of one chap who had had eight flats on this twelve hundred mile stretch, I thought with uneasiness, "This is the Alaska Highway."

We had hardly gone five miles until we met a man who was fixing a flat. He was *five* miles from surcease — we had 1195 miles yet to go. I was not worried about a flat as such. I was thinking about the scheduling of our meetings. Suppose we should have a flat tire on a remote stretch, we might be held up a couple of days. I could not then visualize the nice spacing of gas and repair stations. The remoteness of the area traversed was uppermost in my mind.

Well, it was rough, and it was more muddy than dusty because of opportune rains. We did not have our first soft tire until the second day near Muncho Lake, when we had already gone four hundred fifty miles and had already crossed the highest point on the highway. That was a good third of the way. After a little more experience I predicted we would have a flat about every four hundred miles, which proved to be the average.

By then, we had had some experience with the number and character of the service stations, and I reached a state of mind in which I enjoyed the trip. A flat tire was simply an incident, and a not very serious incident, of travel in this extensive land.

Somebody has remarked that the trip is monotonous. There was some repetition in the general character of the scenery. But for me there was always a sharp sense of expectancy and always the feeling, as I looked out across vast undrained flats of small-growth trees, "There is nothing over there; nothing of man, no trails, no cabins, no concentrations." Out there one would really be on his own. There was no monotony, rather a kind of fearsomeness at the thought of such vastnesses. It would be hard going through some of those trackless muskegs. And where would a person be going?

There was the problem of namelessness. How could one go to a place that had no name? Does man dilute these feelings of boundlessness by affixing names? In a sense, yes. When a place or spot is named (even a remote mountain) it becomes map-able, and the blank spots on the map fill up. The unknown becomes known. Travel becomes a matter of proceeding from known to known. This is what we did on this trip with our maps. But out there — almost everywhere, away from the road, was the unknown. The mind thrilled to the endless blank spaces alongside.

Of course, there was repetition. I recall regular successions of green forest followed by gray-black fire-killed trees. The first massive gray area left me shocked and aghast. It was succeeded by the balm of a healthy, living forest. No one was really deprived by the fire, because obviously no one was using these forests, and clearly never had. Maybe they were not usable, maybe they were not economic. The fires as yet seemed to have no importance or significance in man's world.

I was impressed with the juxtaposition of the living and the dead. Along the highway death succeeded life, or life succeeded death. There was a certain rhythm to it. Maybe that was the way of any *great* wilderness. In these alternations of the green and the gray, I began to see a pattern. Maybe a forest always reached a climax of growth or of fire only to enter a decline. Maybe this was the way of all life. I began, in the vastness, to see ecology on a horizontal scale. There came, after a while, a kind of buoyancy to it. I knew that farther out along the road, life would alternate with the gray hulks through which we were passing. There came to be none of the sadness one feels at a fire or bug-kill in a circumscribed area. Here my mind was free to travel unhampered by assocations with familiar country. Our bodies were moving forward too – a steady two hundred fifty to three hundred miles a day and there was no returning or covering the same ground. There were repeats of some of these burns and kills, but they had boundaries, and their limits were always marked ultimately by nature's vitality. Here, on the earth's face, on a scale as comparably vast as the Grand Canyon, were the workings of ecology. Life did not persist forever up here. Does it anywhere? Nor did death. It was here for us to see. Broad bands of existence and of demise spelled out for us basic rhythms of the earth cover.

It was late June. It was early for many flowers. The desolation of the deadened areas was bleak at first, until we were galvanized by the alternations of green and drab. But we were to observe, later, on our trip up the Yukon from Dawson to Whitehorse, that even the desolation was not absolute. Somewhere along the Yukon, we glanced across a flat to an upland waste which had been seared with fire. There was a slight pinkish glow on the ground, amidst the starkness of the lifeless trees. Remembering the pink rock in Glacier Park last year, I thought that the glow must be caused by the color of exposed rock.

But this time it was not rock, but the bloom of living plants, millions of them – come to heal the earth which had been blackened by fire. We were to see it many times, this blooming of fireweed, in these cindery wastes – a few square feet, an acre, a few acres, and in spots a whole hillside – hundreds of acres – warmly flushed with the bloom of this beautiful plant.

We learned that the rhythms of life do not proceed in a

214

stark succession of single waves from blight to resurgence. In between were wavelets and riffles following in the troughs of the waves. Wavelets of fireweed brought a frail and fleeting glory to the hulks of the trees, while their cones were opening, and their seeds spreading, and the new seedlings were taking hold following the fire.

And so death and the "monotony," became a relative thing and we too were caught up on a wave of understanding. Is there ever really any death? An individual may die. But the great processes go on. Ecology works like yeast. Here in the wastes of the subarctic some of the greatest glories of our trip followed quickly the holocaust of fire. Fireweed we had seen before — single plants, sparsely blooming. Here it blanketed the countryside filling in the blasted areas between the zones of living forest.

On our trip we saw and crossed some of the continent's great rivers, including the Columbia and Mississippi on our return, but none gave us a greater thrill than the Liard, the Yukon, and the Fraser. The first two had a massive, quick-running, powerful appearance. Each carried a heavy, cloudy load of silt. Both were broad and silent where we saw them, although at a few spots the Yukon was broken with islands. But the impression of silent power in the hurried currents of the Liard and Yukon was overwhelming. The Columbia at Portland and the Mississippi at Memphis had by contrast a languorous mood.

The Yukon and Liard were not "civilized" streams; they arose in back country. They flowed through some of the remotest land on the continent. The Mackenzie, for which the Liard was one of the main tributaries, emptied into the Arctic

Ocean and the Yukon, into the Bering Sea. The Liard and Yukon were powerful wild rivers which served the glaciers and the unapproachable north country, and their surging muddy currents reflected this role.

The Fraser we saw in its canyon setting in western British Columbia. It was a clear, rowdy, powerful river whose long canyon was used by two railroads and a highway. The river and its canyon dominated all the works of man and in fact made them possible. There was no other way down through that part of British Columbia except by the canyon of "the mighty Fraser."

We crossed several large tributaries of the Yukon, such as the White and Stewart Rivers, whose sources reached back to the glaciers of the Saint Elias Range. At this season the rivers were low and threads of water snaked through broad expanses of rock bars. Some of the bridges were two and three hundred yards long and the total width of the braided streamlets was only thirty or forty feet. But those vast rock bars had been laid down by mighty currents from spring rains and the melt of the snow and glaciers, when the whole bed was a gray, opaque, and turbulent torrent bearing a saturated load of silt, gravel, and stones. The Liard *did* get out of bounds as we were leaving Alaska, and hundreds of motorists were held up for several days while repairs were being made to the road.

There were countless small lakes and ponds all across central and western Canada and along the Alaska Highway. There were also some very large lakes – Rainy Lake in Minnesota, from which we departed with Ernest Oberholtzer, and the many somber arms and expanses of the rain and fog-shrouded Lake of the Woods.

216

There were some great lakes along the Alaska Highway. Muncho Lake is celebrated throughout Canada for its jade-green color. Then there was the clear, wind-tossed Teslin Lake which reached along the highway for eighty miles. It was long enough to catch the winds, and its shore where we stopped was piled high with tangles of soft, silvery driftwood. The Kluane we saw in subdued blue tones against a background of mountains. It had a wondrous, dreamy appeal.

Wonder Lake in McKinley Park had a certain dour beauty. Its setting was in the low tundra country of the Kantishna drainage some thirty miles from the base of Mount McKinley. Around its shores was a scattered fringe of trees. Its glory was its nearness to Denali where its reflections multiplied the grandeur of that stupendous peak. Except for Denali, Wonder Lake had some of the starkness of a painting by Grant Wood.

Passage through the Rockies was not exciting. There were no high passes. The two highest points on the entire Alaska Highway were roughly a thousand feet lower than New Found Gap (5048 feet) in the Great Smokies.

But after leaving Whitehorse, we began to see ahead a long chain of mountains whose high, icy peaks were eye-catching. We had seen glaciers before but these glaciers seemed to enshroud many of the highest peaks, and I knew that we must be glimpsing the Saint Elias Range.

But one can never perceive true relationships in strange country. These mountains were not as close as expected. Between us and this great range were wide expanses of muskeg and rushing streams, making the mountains seem so small when viewed from the minimizing distances of this vast land and so forbidding when close by. We never got close to the Saint Elias

217

Range. There were always great stretches of intervening land. But our very distance from the mountains accented their huge range and great height. In time they filled the western horizon and we drove parallel to them for better than a day. There were massive fluted slopes reaching up to endless snowy pyramids. Through an opening we would see more peaks – higher and more untouchable and encased in gleaming shrouds of white. I am sure that one of those blinding pyramids which we glimpsed far behind the front range, standing in detached grandeur, was Mount Logan, one of the giant peaks of the continent.

Then came the Dezadeash Range of lesser height but equal beauty and then farther away and with a mightiness of their own, the Wrangell Mountains.

But these glorious spectacles were no preparation for Mount McKinley. I had seen scores of photographs of it. I knew it was the central feature of the east and west extending Alaska Range. In the photos, it always had a kind of diffused quality, because of its broken north slope, and because it seemed to have no central eye-catching pyramid.

I left Fairbanks by train in the rain. Anne and Ober had left the day before by car. I met them at McKinley Park station. It was raining there and it rained lightly as we traveled west. After awhile in a flat area we looked ahead and saw a car stopped amid surrounding brush. As we caught up, several of its occupants had gotten out and had walked fifty yards or so into the muskeg. Superintendent Oscar Dick murmured something about Mount McKinley. We looked and saw nothing but low peaks and a belt of clouds above. And then, we saw a glowing patch of white high above the belt of clouds. It was too brilliant and too solid for mist, but it couldn't be a mountain! No

218

mountain, nothing as solid as a mountain, could be that high above the plane of the earth!

The clouds shifted and we saw another patch of white and we became believers. It was Denali, "the High One," the name given by the Indians. We were denied the full view for awhile longer. We drove down the winding Kantishna road and then up the private road to Camp Denali.

We were to see the mountain under varying light – at midnight, at darkening twilight, before three o'clock in the morning, and in bright sunlight. Never did it seem so aloof, so unbelievable, so non-earthly as when we first saw it across the muskeg that late afternoon.

McKinley must be one of the great mountain spectacles of the world. When we were meeting in the lodge, Wilderness Society Council members would continually look out to see if Denali were showing. If they were sitting with their backs to the window, they would twist around so they could look out. The mountain was photographed at all hours. Olaus got up at midnight so he could catch it with the moonrise. Our group is a sophisticated one. Yet this spectacle held their unabashed interest for the five days we were there.

Denali is not a gaunt, sharp pyramid. It is so huge and sprawling, it has a baffling quality. It has the unity of a crowd, but not the sharpness of a single individual. But its loftiness when the clouds were low – more hanging or floating far above the earth than a part of it – always drew our attention. Its brilliant, faceted whiteness towering over every surrounding was matchless. Indeed, for us and all people the mountain is *Denali, the High One.*

Around Fairbanks we heard that the caribou were moving

through the Park. We had not expected to see them. We who work at conservation matters throughout the year, full or even part time, need contact with the wilderness. We need to get our batteries recharged with sights of some of the massive continental phenomena. I was fearful that the thin chance of seeing caribou would vanish. But at last Anne, Ober, and I were together and starting out toward Camp Denali. We rounded a bend in the road and spotted a movement on the slopes above — three lone caribou. The wondrous story of the caribou and of their migrations came alive for me in the sight of those three startled animals. We saw more that afternoon with their fantastic antlers and many, many more when we took our field trip on the Fourth of July. But this glimpse of three was like looking through a telescope into the heart of the Northland.

On the Fourth of July we saw them in substantial herds, milling about. These animals had something of the color of the tundra. At a distance they were hard to distinguish from the landscape, even when someone pointed them out. Then suddenly the earth would start to flow and one realized that a group of them had taken off with that strange and exciting fluid motion.

How do these animals differ from others? What impulsions gear those great migrations? Hunger, I suppose, and an instinct to preserve their range or at least an impulsion to move on when it becomes depleted. But why do they move together in such great numbers? People have become dependent upon each other because of specialization. But there is no apparent specialization of activity among the caribou. Each could maintain life a long time alone and satisfactorily. I did see one all alone on the high ridge back of Camp Denali. Was he a caribou outcast or was he a Daniel Boone venturing out on his own? Is the migration a frightening thing for them like a sort of Columbus voyage? Is it so momentous and debilitating that each needs the sustaining warmth of the presence of hundreds and even thousands of others? Is life in the far north so austere that they must be fortified by the proximity of others?

I also wanted to see a grizzly bear. I remembered the passage in the Lewis and Clark Journals, how astonished they were when they first saw these fearsome creatures. They are one of the earth's great mammals. We missed seeing a grizzly on the Fourth of July, although we did see a golden eagle tearing mightily at a caribou carcass which a grizzly had recently quitted. On the return that day to Camp Denali, we saw about fifty yards away, a bald eagle. Our list of wild things seen had mounted. But we had not seen a grizzly.

On the way out of the Park two days later, this particular wish was granted. Along the road we saw Andy Russell, a great hunter, naturalist, and conservationist from British Columbia, sitting with his field glasses. I stopped to chat with him. He was watching an old grizzly sow and two cubs. With the glasses we could easily see her busily moving amongst some willows. She was a light, tawny brown and her pelt was so thick and velvety, only the more obvious structure of her body was perceivable. We could see the head, legs, and the swelling across the shoulders and that was about all. After watching awhile I could make out two darker bundles of fur scrambling about her feet and sometimes behind her. These were the cubs. The overall effect, at that distance, of adult and cubs alike, was of big, woolly caterpillars crawling busily about. The similarity carried to the undulations of the body. We watched for a long time.

That night we stayed in Charley Ott's cabin fourteen miles

222

down the Denali Highway from Park Headquarters. It was in an exquisite setting. As we walked in the front door we faced a picture-window through which we could see a gem of a lake, clean and forest surrounded, and beyond that a slope of naked mountain tundra. Charley said an avalanche had killed fifteen caribou up there in the spring and that that morning six grizzlies had been seen at the carcasses. I swept the slopes with the glasses in vain that evening, but the next morning, as we were getting breakfast, I spotted two grizzlies moving about with great concentration and purpose although I could not ascertain the purpose. They were agile, powerful animals, and moved as vigorously up slope as when they were descending.

In the Park we also saw Dall sheep above us on barren slopes.

Moose were numerous. We saw them frequently along the roads. They did not seem disturbed by a car, although they would usually move on if we stopped. We saw several foxes in the Park and once on the Alaska Highway a lynx crossed the pavement ahead of us. The sight of this latter animal was thrilling indeed.

A continual joy to which I never became accustomed was the twenty-four hours of near daylight. Even Mardy Murie, when she packed for this trip to Alaska, forgot and put a flashlight into her luggage. Anne left our bird book at home and put in a book on the stars! I don't believe we saw a single star until we returned to the "lower forty-eight." Folks inquired how we slept. I didn't have too much trouble sleeping. I was unaffected by the psychological role which darkness plays in preparing one for sleep. At home we might sit around until dark to start a meeting, but not in Alaska. Meetings in Alaska had to start by the clock for real darkness never came.

On the last evening at Camp Denali, George Marshall suggested a hike. He and Anne and I started out at ten p.m. for the ridge back of the camp. There was still a pinkish glow on McKinley from the setting sun. At eleven, the glow was still there, and the moon startled us as it slipped brilliantly from behind a lesser peak. Its trajectory was flat and low on the horizon and it appeared and reappeared three times as we watched. At eleven p.m., I took a photograph in color of the moon and Mount McKinley, the latter still slightly aglow from the sun. Earlier in the week I had poked my camera out of our cabin door at 2:45 a.m. and photographed McKinley, which was already a shining white from the rising sun.

But the long days, we were told, were balanced by twenty-four hours of darkness in winter, and in bad weather the confinement to houses in unbroken darkness was depressing.

Our hike that night was truly a joy — more rewarding perhaps than our daytime trip up the same slope, because our attention was focused that evening on the Alaska Range. We had no difficulty working out through the muskeg to the foot of the ridge. In the boggy area the mosquitoes swarmed about us, but, as in Minnesota, they did not seem particularly vicious. We would brush them off and move along. We would climb awhile rather steeply and then turn and stand for a look at Denali. We had forgotten the moon and when we first saw it appearing from behind a peak, we thought momentarily we were witnessing an explosion of cosmic origin. There was an unsettling fraction of a moment before we identified it for what it was — the moon.

One of the striking areas which we saw in Alaska was midway on the Denali Highway. The road rose to an eminence.

Below us in silver braids lay the Nenana River. This was not a glacial stream and the water was clear and brilliant. The silver of the stream was interlaced with the green of the banks and of little emerald islets. Much of the Alaska that we saw had something of the rawness of its great peaks and of its distant north. On the Nenana, water and vegetation at this spring season blended in as fair a sight as we had ever seen. Then we began to look across brown moors to some of the massive and imposing glaciers of the continent. But the Nenana did not arise in these and had a clear beauty which was a rarity in the Alaska we saw.

I have been looking at a map of Alaska. The roads center around the southeast quarter between and around Fairbanks on the north and Anchorage and Valdez on the south. We were on most of the roads around Fairbanks. People were flying almost daily to Point Barrow, Kotzebue, and other far points. There came a feeling that Alaska was not as large as I had thought.

When I read several years ago Adolph Murie's *The Wolves of Mount McKinley* I received the impression that Alaska was a boundless land with innumerable packs of wolves. Now I wonder. Even the Park, large as it is, is not large enough to contain its wolves and it has been proposed to add some tracts on the north in order to try to bring within the Park boundaries the full range of these free-running animals.

Much of Mount McKinley Park is above timber line. Because of its openness it seemed less than its three thousand square miles. When the Council members hiked on the Fourth of July in several parties, we saw nearly every person from the visitors' center. I wish I might have hiked that day; I might have felt its vastness more, had I had more of it underfoot. But the feeling

225

which possesses me, as I think back on it here at home, is that the Park is not limitless. I had rather expected to feel otherwise. The Park would benefit by the inclusion of much of the area south of the summit of the Alaska Range. There seems to be no compelling reason why the reservation should occupy only the north slopes of that range.

Some of my impressions are contradictory. I did get an impression of vastness as we drove through Canada toward Alaska. I got it again as we drove the Taylor Highway to Dawson. But now I am subdued by the residual impression that this vast country is finite after all.

I wish I did not have this response to my experiences there. I do not want to talk about it to others. But I do want to set down what I am thinking for reexamination later. In any event, on our next trip to Alaska we should hike more and perhaps take some of it by canoe. We should try to feel the ruggedness and austerities of that great land.

Perhaps it doesn't pay to find out too much about a place. I had the same feeling of finiteness at the Oregon Dunes. Unique as they are, how little will be saved. In the redwood country the parks were magnificent, or perhaps the trees in the parks were. But I carried away disturbing impressions of those scalped hills nearby, of the ubiquitous sawdust burners at the mills, and of the dizzy, frenetic endless chain of trucks carrying felled redwood trees to the market. There is no vastness any more, nothing unknown or "lost behind the ranges." I returned depressed by these wholesale cuttings. If it is bad now, it will be worse forty years hence when there will likely be twice as many people competing for harshly reduced resources.

On our return trip from Alaska we drove the Taylor

Highway from Tok Junction to Dawson to Whitehorse. I can't remember very much about the first part of the trip other than proceeding up a small creek, the bed of which had been worked over by dredges – every foot of it. It must have been a very rich creek. Later we came down to West Fork and saw a large dredge systematically rooting up its bed and discharging the spoil in great windrows of rock. It gave us a residual taste of the enormous bustle and hopes of adventuring men sixty years before. Then each man was on his own. This huge dredge had reduced the take to a mathematical probability based on a huge turnover of material. There are still a few people who own claims here and there, but the great stir and ferment which gripped this country sixty years ago is gone.

After we left this stream we climbed again into wide-open mountain tundra. It was there that the Alaska-Yukon border was touched by civilization momentarily. On a bleak and lonely upland, devoid of trees, we came to a building starkly prominent on the open landscape – the Canadian customs. What a place for the boundary! Never have I seen anything which etched more dramatically the puniness of man's world on the vast expanses of the earth than this petty outpost. It is a fitting commentary upon the sheer barrenness of the country that this building was closed and people were referred to the customs office in Dawson – sixty miles away.

But this extensive world of high bald hills and domes had a profound fascination. I have been above timber line on other occasions, from the savanna-like grasses on Popocatépetl in Mexico to the grassed barrens of Tenaya Pass in the Sierras. I have seen it in the Flat Tops of Colorado, on Sheep Mountain and the Cloud Peaks of Wyoming, and at the top of the Chinese Wall in the Bob Marshall Wilderness Area in Montana. I have even experienced it along the Presidential Range in New Hampshire. In those places there were other mountains around. There was a certain intimacy to the experience.

But on that lonely border country, we were at the top of a series of rolling mountains. The arctic world seemed to reach out illimitably in every direction. There was loneliness and a complete absence of man far and beyond any experience I had had before. Ours was almost the only presence. Here was an aloofness beyond fathoming. We were on the edge of a wilderness seemingly without bound which reached in ever wilder and more primitive aspects half a thousand miles to the Arctic Ocean. Alone in such space a man would become a prophet or a saint or he would go crazy. It is no wonder that all of the great religions have been born and nurtured in such surroundings. And the awful aloneness of the wilderness to which Jesus repaired in his hours of agony took on profound meaning.

The hills rolled off in the haze and mists to unseen and uncramped horizons. It was a scene and an experience without parallel. Here was the haunting untouchableness of land, as yet unharnessed and subdued by man. We reached out in our spirits to this misty amplitude, which was blurred by its own vastness. Up there, every point of the compass beckoned. There was nothing in focus, nothing to pinpoint it on the maps of mankind. And our souls swelled and grew, trying to reach out on all sides.

The thin tenuousness of the vegetation creeping behind the shelter of rocks and venturing out on these windy downs gripped us. Here and there a flower bloomed in a sparse and lonely glory. Here the earth's poverty was so desolate that no trees found lodgment — only these doughty plants which

228

exploded in one burst of bloom and then clung, dormant through another year of cold.

I did not understand the functioning of life up there. We saw a surprising number of individual flowers in bloom, and mosses and lichens. Except for the thin thread of the road and that isolated building there was nothing of man's world to complicate the picture. Man's transforming and destructive influence was noteworthy for its absence. From that point north there were no roads. Man penetrated, if at all, by planes or river or more appropriately in the winter by dog team. To the north, man and nature met in a stand-off. Not that he could not prevail if it were economic or militarily desirable to do so. But in the normal economy few men are tempted to go up there. A few scientists, a few trappers and prospectors, and a few natives who had adjusted completely to its rigors, and that is all. We were profoundly touched by this threshold visit to another world.

In the Klondike days, the rivers were the highways. There was variation, when the weather turned cold and the dog teams were used. Highways have not been and are not yet the major factor in Alaskan transport. There is a rail line from Anchorage to Fairbanks and a narrow gauge from Skagway to Whitehorse. Today, the air is the "highway." The air is a pervasive thing which reaches every corner of the country.

The motor car is not the dominant medium of transportation. It was this thought that made the view north from those boundary domes so enthralling. True, it was only five hundred miles to the Arctic Ocean. But beyond where we stood, where the automobile could not be used, the distance seemed terrific. It was a world which was closed to us.

On the map the area of the upper Koyukuk above Wiseman, which Bob Marshall made so appealing in his writings, is actually limited in miles. It is the inaccessibility and the lack of facilities on the ground that make it seem boundless.

So, in thinking back on Alaska my thoughts have a curious ambivalence. It seemed a huge land and yet as I study the maps, I am appalled at how much of it we were able to thread because we were in a car. I am aware that we did not traverse the areas between the roads — the Alaska Range, the Wrangell Mountains, the Saint Elias Range, and the misty valleys between. Although we found the boundaries of much of the geography, I am happy that the vegetation, animal life, and ecology remain a mystery.

21

W E HAD further notable experiences in Oregon and California on our return from Alaska.

The Oregon Dunes were not as sheer and barren as I had expected. Vegetation, I found, is one of the charms of the dunes and the amount is one of their measures. But it was the sand which most delighted me. We left the car at the end of a hard, clay-surfaced road and were immediately in the sand. It collapsed and shifted under our feet. It was early in the morning and I had had a good night's sleep. I thought we would proceed vigorously up onto the dunes. I had not taken two steps before I knew better.

We followed first a kind of roadway. In the blazing sun the sand had no consistency. Progress was by a kind of short-paced hobble. We could not stride out and shove with the toes. We learned immediately to shorten our pace. We had to keep our bodies over our feet. It was not completely frustrating, because we did make progress. But the sand was terribly restrictive. What started out as a lark became heavy, slow business.

We reached a low point on the sandy roadway and saw a big dune ahead. I wanted to climb it, so we bore to the left through patches of saw grass. The wind had whipped the fronds of the grass about, and the tips had lightly marked the sand in delicately beautiful circular patterns. These sheer markings were as fleeting as they were delicate. One surge of wind and they were gone. We had walked boldly off the road, straight for the dune. As always in new country I looked for landmarks and then noted our tracks in the sand. I said blithely to Anne,

"If we lose our bearings we can always follow our tracks back to the car."

A couple of hours later our tracks had been obliterated.

We started straight up the dune. It was unbelievably tiring. To ease the numbness in our thighs, we started on a slant across the face. It was not too high — perhaps two hundred feet, but it taxed us heavily. At the crest was one of those sheer, clean, knife-edged combs. Even on top, the sand gave way beneath our feet and we progressed by short, flat-footed steps.

Up there the sun's rays beat mercilessly on the sand and I began to be aware of some of the forces which affect the existence and shape of dunes. There was considerable moisture in the sand. It was only on the surface that the sand was completely dry. The dampness was the only cohesive force. Each grain was a unit, and when the moisture was drawn off into the atmosphere, the grains began to slide downhill until they reached a more shallow slope and repose.

On the east and south slopes the surface was alive with

moving sand grains. The movement of one disturbed others. Perhaps its weight overrode the others or perhaps it "pulled the rug" from under those above. The path of one grain quickly became a flowing current. There was no stability anywhere. The first flow followed a narrow, fluted channel. But other channels formed to the right and left. The ridges between caved in and the channel widened. What started as narrow, graceful flutings quickly spread under the drying sun into wide shallow saucers of disturbance. Each disturbed area broadened laterally and ultimately moved upward to the head of the dune and stole its crest.

But how under such constant and widespread movement could the dune maintain its shape? How could it hold that knife-edged crest? Why did not all the dunes become low and rounded? And then we perceived another phenomenon. The knife edge was not as clean and sharp as it had first appeared. As I studied it, I realized it was bathed in a kind of haze. The winds from the ocean side were picking up dry, light grains on that side and blowing them up the slope — some even over the top. What was lost to the sun and gravity on the sunny side was being restored by the wind on the ocean side. And this was how the dunes traveled — not from their foundation but along their surfaces, which were never in repose. The crest of the dune was constantly being added to, grain by grain, on the one side. It was constantly being diminished and lowered grain by grain, on the other.

These were the dunes. Given the proper ingredients, light sand and exposure to sun and winds, they were never in repose. They were moving, moving — not slowly in timeless heavings, but ceaselessly, restlessly, minute by minute, second by second — altering their shape — changing their area of occupancy —

233

overflowing themselves, overriding everything before them.

On the inland side we saw forests half buried – the sand high on their trunks, the upper limbs deadened and stark. The dunes were moving toward a highway, and threatened to bury it. This was an indignity which man could not abide. He would stop those dunes! So with Scotch broom and a beach grass imported from Holland he was undertaking to arrest this inexorable movement by plantings on the beach and on the slopes. As we looked down from above we could see the geometric patterns, the checkerboards of beach grass with which the area had been planted. I have no idea whether the movement will be arrested. A young forester who was in charge of the work said it would be stopped. My covert wish was that the movement would not be stopped. And as I think back, of that fine haze of sand which softened by ever so little the sharp, knife edge of the dune crest, I wondered if it would be stopped.

As we drove on down the coast there was a screen of trees between the road and sand. But through the screen we could see a monstrous, straw-colored skyline. This was not a distant skyline keeping a decent distance as in the mountains. This was a near, almost frightening presence, moving defiantly into the forests and the economy of man. One federal agency imbued with economics was trying to stem this slow engulfing tide of sand. Another, more flexible, and appreciating the sly forces at work, said it would move the road.

It all reminded me of a quatrain from Tennyson's *In Memoriam:*

> "The hills are shadows, and they flow
> From form to form, and nothing stands;
> They melt like mist, the solid lands,
> Like clouds they shape themselves and go."

234

REDWOODS

From the dunes we went to something more rooted — the giant redwoods of California. We shall remember them as long and as gratefully as we shall remember Denali. We spent a half day in those groves and had to tear ourselves away. We could have spent a week without being satiated. Never have I seen living things so great, so perfect, so untouchable. Man with his customary self-importance has marked some of them with his signs. One is called "Founders Tree" — not in honor of the tree, but in honor of those men and women who appreciated the trees enough to protect them. And so the trees themselves are used to foster man's little vanities.

But the groves, back in the forest where the trails gave out, where folks seldom go, gave rise to feelings of utter insufficiency. Such repose, such perfection, so beyond reach! We felt no hostility, but there was no warmth. Nothing reached out a hand to lead us through this experience. We were like the ants which dodge about at the feet of men. Here, ant-like, we dodged around at the feet of these noble trees.

They were taller than many of our buildings and more shapely and more impervious to erosion and decay. Fire, they had withstood; life, they still had. They were older by millenia than any man and outdated many of his civilizations. The industrial age was a mere scratch in the bark of one of these giants. Christianity? Many of these trees were old when Jesus walked the earth.

Their size and age, symmetry and aplomb, produced

profound humility in us. In the groves we found a hushed gloaming. It was a hush that soothed us. But there was also space of such incredible dimensions we could not touch it. Giant ferns and oxalis covered the ground. We went places which seemed never to have been disturbed. Even the ground cover belonged to another world.

We looked through natural vistas and saw and felt the quiet and serenity of these great trees. They rose like columns all around us. But like columns we had never seen, they supported vaultings of living green. Here was symmetry and grace, before men had even coined the words. Here was silence and insouciance before men had given them names. Anne and I were quiet — what could we say? What could anyone say?

But in the early morning, before the fog had lifted and before the sun's rays and light had drifted in, out of the unreachable gloom above us, we had heard the spirited joyous notes of the winter wren. And I thought, "Sprite that he is, he can compass this experience better than we." We try to find words to express the awesome hollowness within us. He turns to song and joy. He is glad to be alive — and so should we be. We felt rebuffed and left out of the colossal, haunting beauty. *He,* tiny being that he was, responded with all his soul and body.

22

COUGAR LAKES
OLYMPIC BEACH
WASHINGTON
MISSOURI RIVER BREAKS
MISSION MOUNTAINS
LINCOLN BACK COUNTRY
MONTANA
1964

O F ALL the recent incidents and experiences the one I cherish most was the sight of twenty-two mountain goats at rest on a snow field high on Nelson Ridge in the Cougar Lakes Limited Area. We had ridden horses up the very steep Thunder Creek trail to a pass. We had passed beds of brilliantly colored wild flowers and had stopped for a drink of sparkling water. Much of the trail had been in a deep forest. But in the little meadows the sun glared down upon us. From the rocky outcrop where we ate lunch we could see cliffs and grassy benches — small clumps of timber, small patches of snow and tiny rills of water gleaming in the sun. At this latitude, eight thousand feet of elevation is perfect goat country. Soon we spotted a lone ram, and a hundred yards over — a nanny and kid. They were restless, moving from the sun into shade. Then they disappeared. The gray rocks which at a distance look like

238

goats refused to move for us. The goats had vanished. Somehow I felt a little lonelier because man himself is a predator.

After lunch Bill Douglas suggested walking up the divide to a grassy bald. The going was steep and hot. I paused to look at the rugged landscape with the binoculars. I thought I might see one or two of the goats which had walked out of our view lower down. I swept the cliffs and benches and then a snow field. I was galvanized by what I saw. The lumps strung across the snow field were not inert boulders. They were goats lying down and at ease. Most of them were in a fairly compact group, but several had isolated themslves from the others. The whole group was strung out over an area one hundred fifty yards long. There were twenty-two in all.

What a spectacle! This Cougar Lakes country is so wild that the sight of goats had become almost commonplace. I had seen the goats on two previous visits. Among them there was no restlessness, no stir − movement to be sure, as the turning of heads − but no fear, no rushing away from us. Bill and I were in full sight. No doubt they could see us, as we saw them. But they were not frightened and were idly glancing about and not searching the area for enemies.

It was like looking into a living room from the street − into the relaxed intimacy of a family group. These goats were at home. We were intruders, but very sympathetic ones. We had no cause to disturb them. We would have liked to get closer for photographs but did not and contented ourselves with an attempt to photograph them through an eyepiece of our binoculars.

One thing was very disturbing. Douglas observed that they were lying only a few yards from the crest of the ridge which was the boundary of the Limited Area. These animals could not exist in a restricted range. Over the course of a summer they needed to move and feed over considerable distance. In the winter migrations they are known to move fifteen miles or more. The construction of truck roads to the foot of the cliffs across the divide, which was in the plans, would box them in. They would lose range and probably lose numbers from crowding and hunting, and the exquisite intimacy of that large family group on the snow field would be broken.

OLYMPIC BEACH

The rendezvous for the second Olympic Beach hike was near the mouth of the Hoh River, across from the Hoh Indian Reservation, near a damp and mosquitoey bog. We walked out to the beach where we chose a camping spot not too far from a huge log at the lip of a slope of gravel which ran down to the water. I sat on a log talking with John Osseward after the salmon bake and watched the waves gradually inching to within ten feet of where we were sitting. It was getting close enough that I was prompted to ask when the tide would crest. The water had already seeped under us through the gravel and had formed a substantial pool much nearer the forest.

We folded our nylon tarp so that half of it served as a ground cloth and the other half could be pulled over us should it rain. Thus we settled in our sleeping bags for the night. At our heads and not more than twenty feet from us was the edge of the Pacific Ocean. The constant roar of the water was punctuated by more intensive bursts as a particularly high wave rolled over on itself and broke. The pounding had a massive quality which engulfed us in a stir of emotion and even trepidation, as surely as thirty feet farther west, we would have been engulfed in water. I remembered only too well the driftwood barriers of six years ago where whole trees six and eight feet in diameter had been flung up on the beach and I was cognizant that we were lying much closer to the water than were those trees.

In the night there came an insistent patter of rain on our tarp and we pulled in our heads like terrapins. The air beneath became close and stuffy and when it seemed we would suffocate, we would stick our heads out and catch the rain in our faces. Then the rain would let up and we would see a star and would strain our red-rimmed eyes in hopes of seeing more. It was a long night on the hard-packed sand and we were damp around the edges. The tarp not only shed water but collected it where it was not properly drained. By morning, the rain which was never very heavy had ceased, and we were not very wet. But we had begun to accumulate into our things the first of the sand we were to collect inadvertently, in spite of all our care, for three days and nights.

Six years ago when we walked the beach from Cape Alava to La Push, the ocean was on our right. This time, as we headed north from the Hoh River, it was on our left. As on the earlier trip, the ocean was still the single overmastering presence. This time we knew something of what we might encounter — the miles' long tangle of driftwood, hard-packed sand, loose-shifting sand, the great jumbles of rock where a headland touched the sea, sea stacks (remnant headlands fantastic in outline and vegetative cover), the filming out of a wave on an almost level beach, tidal pools with gorgeous anemones and orange starfish.

These things we had seen before. What was new were freshwater streams, clear and clean, flowing into the ocean. On the previous trip, we had been forced to drink from amber pools. This time we crossed many streams of fresh water, two or three of them too wide to jump.

We camped one night just north of Mosquito Creek. Those who had tents were independent of the need for driftwood props. The others of us improvised fantastic shelters with the aid of driftwood. At Mosquito Creek we found an arching tree limb over which we spread the tarp and we had good shelter and good drainage. I never quite mastered the art of sleeping on the sand. The hip holes were either too deep and angular, or not deep enough.

The members of the party enjoyed assembling at night in tight rings around the campfire while the ocean pounded at their backs. They loved the ocean, the hard hiking, the creaking of the straps on their packs, the long vistas, but they liked to get together and discuss the concerns of men. This was the ambivalence of man and the earth at its very best.

I liked to look at figures on the beach against the evening light. They were so tiny they were almost lost in the great scene. I liked the surf birds congregating in the water, half salt and half fresh at the mouth of a stream. Mosquito Creek, where it ran into the sea, cut a little channel in the sand and rippled over the rocks in its bed, but lost its identity finally in the waves. I watched this creek at the end of its journey, where it mingled with sea and awaited the long cycles of wind and weather which would carry it again in tiny droplets back onto the land. I stood there long minutes thinking of the history of the earth — the primordial envelope of clouds around a sizzling orb, the torrential rains slicing and cutting down the earth and gathering in streams and flowing in countless cycles to the sea. This scene at the mouth of this stream was small enough to take in. But small as it was the flow had the power to cut a definite channel through the final sand beds.

Unlike our trip in 1958, on this one we had nearly as much of the land as of the sea. The headlands were more abrupt, and the tides less convenient. The weather was more inclement and the beautiful headlands became nightmares of gumbo — treacherous and slippery. Under the ferns and great trees, there were endless trenches of mud. In the ubiquitous shade, the great rains soaked into the soil and flowed nowhere. We were brought face to face, and boot to mud, with a rain forest.

Even at the end of the hike, where the Park Service had provided shallow boxes filled with earth for steps, and where there was a mile or more of board walk, the going was slippery. This ubiquitous mud I had never experienced before, except in the mires of the Smokies near Indian Gap over forty years ago. On top of one headland we had to wade a stream of surprising width. Even getting down to it was an ordeal, over an eight-foot gooey drop. Everybody waded; most removed their boots. Along the bluffs above the beach the banks of ferns were enormous, and the screen of ferns and trees between us and the sea was like Japanese art.

We descended a gravelly path to the driftwood and the strand. There in august surroundings we rested, sharing experiences with folks who had ranged the world, folks with free, questioning minds. It was a glimpse of the promise life holds for everyone. Physical exertion, broken by periods of reflection and enjoyment with like-minded people. Such people were there in numbers. In age, from six to seventy-six — twenty-five were over sixty — tough and competent, and not overstretching themselves. The wilderness may tax the lazy and overawe the uninitiated, but it will not be denied to staunch souls who want it.

243

MISSOURI RIVER BREAKS

Our second exhilaration was as much an emotion as it was an observation. I am thinking of our float trip down the upper Missouri River. In reaching it Anne and I had driven down the valley of the Gallatin River. Its wide curves, the stretches of grassy valley snuggled into its bends, its uncrowdedness and its swift-running clarity render it one of the most gorgeous rivers we have seen. All of it should be in a national park, as is already its upper end. The water is dazzling and alive.

I was puzzled: how could water so transparent and pure make up in time a part of the muddy Missouri? Our trip, on to Helena that day and on to Fort Benton and beyond on the next, became a continuing inquiry. We had descended the Gallatin River almost to its mouth where it joined the Jefferson and Madison Rivers to become the Missouri. After leaving the Gallatin we crossed both the Jefferson and Madison shortly above Three Forks. All three rivers were clear. Two or three times we saw the Missouri at a distance below the forks. Everywhere, except at the upper end of the Canyon Ferry Reservoir, where high winds were stirring the mud in the shallows, its water had a sheer transparency. When I saw the bronze tawniness of the water at the upper end of Canyon Ferry, I thought "This is where the muddiness begins." But it was fresh and clear again as we drove beside the river below Helena. It seemed attractive and clear when we stopped at the little park at Fort Benton, although the beginnings of pollution and turbidity were present. We caught at Fort Benton the odor of raw sewage. At Virgelle Ferry, a few miles farther downstream, I detected for the first time a sallow cloudiness to the water.

244

And so at Virgelle Ferry, where we entered the Missouri River, it had become, if not the "Big Muddy," at least the Slightly Muddy. I had seen enough to conclude that in this area of low rainfall and scant run-off, this nebulous opacity was probably due to other causes than farming. I looked at the dry, loose, silty clay across from the Great White Wall where we had lunch and where we hiked for a mile or so back into the hinterland. It seemed clear that in periods of high water, the Missouri itself tore loose the silt along its banks. There were numerous evidences of the high water from the flood of a few months earlier. There was proof in the very shallows of the river bed. All of these pointed to the conclusion that somewhere between the canyon below Helena, and the stretch of river we floated, soil conditions marked the river for a muddy destiny whether man was present or not.

It was not just the river and its ofttimes spectacular banks which I enjoyed most. I had a deep awareness that physically the country we were going through had changed but little since Lewis and Clark had ascended this same stretch nearly one hundred sixty years earlier. It was like living a bit of history and knowing at the time that it was history.

Of course we were descending the river and not ascending it. We were, unfortunately, using a power boat. We were not laboriously lining it along the banks. We saw little wild game — only a few antelope standing alertly in grass on the rounded knobs not far below the Virgelle Ferry and quite a few great blue herons among the shallows lower down. Lewis and Clark, on the other hand, saw much game — grizzlies, antelope, elk, bison, which they hunted and upon which they lived. They came along in mid-July, we in early August. We, fresh from offices and desks, blistered under the pitiless sun. They were

245

tanned and bearded and were cooled by the water as they lined their boats. We ate sandwiches and fruit and drank ice water. They ate "immensely of meat," reserving their flour and parched meal and corn for the mountains ahead of them. They no doubt drank from the Missouri itself, although they were adept at spotting the springs and side streams which brought fresh water to the river.

They were uncertain and questioning — not sure of their route. We were floating downstream over a stretch of river which had been widely used for a century and a half. The Lewis and Clark diorama in the museum in Helena had disclosed the crudest of boats, makeshift tools, and weather-beaten faces and clothes. It bespoke the herculean problem of keeping dry their powder, their few instruments, their journals, and precious specimens. We were blithely descending under an almost cloudless sky, and rubbing on sunburn lotion, and wearing dark glasses to alleviate the stringencies of the day.

All these and other things stood out in stark contrast between our little excursion and the epochal journey of Lewis and Clark. But there were points of similarity. They were seeing this for the first time. So were we. In the interim man had passed it by. Except for the scarcity of game and the occasional presence of grazing cattle, the landscape had changed but little. Only the Indians had viewed this country even fleetingly, before they, the first white men, were to see it. We were seeing the same cliffs and walls for the first time, unchanged (as man marks change) from the Lewis and Clark days.

There were the same caving banks along the river, the same grass covered domes, the same grassy benches, where Lewis must have seen his first goats, the same far-extending white walls of hardened silt or rock, the same pinnacles and

246

battlements, the same holes eroded through thin walls, intricate carvings which at a distance looked like Egyptian reliefs, the same black extrusions almost as thin as knife blades extending across country, the same pedestals of soft rock capped with flat disks of harder rock, the same rocky castles and compounds; similar benches of cottonwoods close to the river and along streams which emptied into it, similar shallows, riffles, and rapids in the river, the same bewildering bends lost in distance, the same sagebrush and willows, pungent berries, and tiny flat valleys and ravines. All of these followed each other in perplexing sequence. They were as new to us as to Lewis and Clark themselves.

It was rough, hot, and in some ways forbidding country. It had to be, to have been once the habitat of goats and grizzlies. May it be preserved for what it is, a remote, fascinating valley, rich with history. And for what it may become again, the home of goats and elk and deer and possibly bison, grizzlies, beaver, and otters. It could then enfold visitors in a present which would also be past and future — and the ageless processes of evolution would have free sway again.

The river and its valley were not as deep as I expected. But when is the unknown quite as expected? The river was wider; the valley was less than canyon-like. If it had been, it would not have been good habitat for game. The Missouri is like its consort — the Mississippi. Both carry their loads of silt which are forever being deposited at unpredictable places. Several times we ran aground in the middle of the stream and the two Bobs hopped out and waded around on the bar getting us afloat. It seemed incongrous, even daring — almost like walking on water — to start walking around in the midst of such a noted stream. But that is the Missouri — huge, uncertain and unpredictable, a worthy drainage for one of the handsomest parts of the continent.

MISSION MOUNTAINS

The east side of the Mission Range was high, steep, rough, and heavily glaciated. It is a narrow range but the country back of its sharp façade is gorgeous. The Missions are not too high, only about 9500 feet. The lakes which average about 6500 feet are timbered around their edges and surrounded by rank vegetation. Timber line appears on the higher slopes. The lakes thus have a fine setting and there is good range for the horses. But on the benches above, trees grew more tentatively and in sparse clumps. Some of the shelves were rich with flowers and the densest stand of bear grass I saw on our whole western trip was not far above Summit Lake.

Climbing the main ridge presented no great problems. Sometimes we had to guess on which side of a rib of rock we should go. Sometimes we inched up a steep-lying snow slope. Sometimes we were on rock cliffs. But the rock was firm and sharp and often fallen into steps. It was exciting and not particularly dangerous, although the slopes were precipitous. We fairly hung over the lake and were never out of sight of it. We were often in sight of four different lakes.

Once we went up an open chimney, from which the views were tremendous. We marked our progress upward by Eagle Pass which was to the west of Summit Lake. Ultimately we were well above it. At that elevation the vegetation was thin, and rocks and talus were everywhere. When we were well up on the side of Mount Harding which jutted a couple of hundred feet above the front divide, we could look down and see three

248

of our companions – tiny figures in a great sweep of broken rock. We could see everything they did, when they rested, when they moved, and which way they went, until descending they were lost in the vastness. Seldom have I climbed where the views were so authoritative.

The summit was a knife edge and we squirmed around one edge of Mount Harding and saw the prodigious view down into the main Flathead Valley with its checkerboard of tiny green-and-tan fields, and the scattering of silvery water-filled potholes which were grouped like craters on the moon. It was dizzying to stand upon the rocky apex of such a sheer rib of mountains.

Perhaps these mountains appealed to me as much for their untrammeled vegetation as for their roughness. There seemed to be no grazing on the east slopes. The flowers were rich and in the glaciated valleys, the trails were thickety. We wound through willow brakes so dense we could not see the horse ahead. I have never seen such trails. They were primitive and notably lacking in maintenance. We walked for miles leading or following our horses because of the tough terrain. The trail worked its way across talus so undisturbed, it could hardly be differentiated. We led our horses up rocky bulges so steep and smooth the horses had to scramble and claw for footing almost like cats. We were told to stay from under them lest they would tumble down upon us. One pack horse lost its footing on the slopes above Lake McDonald and had to be cut loose to avoid dragging another horse with him.

Then I watched in horror as Bud Cheff led two pack horses up bare rock. They were heavily loaded and were tied tandem. One staggered, lost his footing, and lunged against the other. I closed my eyes. But by a miracle they caught themselves and

249

were dragged onto a spot of safety. Scrambling horses in such a place were like exploding dynamite. Farther along, the trail climbed a mountain face along rocky shelves one above the other. There we moved our horses two at a time. There was something unnerving in the sight of horses jostling each other on crags perpendicularly above us.

Bud Cheff told about returning through the Missions from the Bob Marshalls. It had started to snow. Night and the temperature settled down. He fought his way one horse at a time to the top of the pass. Had he waited until daylight he would have lost them all.

He told of hunting back of McDonald Peak. They were camped on one side of a stream. Snow was deep. One morning they saw eight grizzlies tramping down the far bank in the snow. Grizzlies now are fewer. They need room to roam. When they are hunted and pressed, they leave. They have to have space. That is why the Mission Mountains and the Lincoln Back Country are so important. They provide suitable range for grizzly bears.

Country like the Missions should never be tamed. It is primitive America almost unchanged.

On the return, we pulled out of one of the cirques through a bleak and rocky pass to a kind of plateau. We rode past several small lakes and came onto a spacious meadow near Mollman Lake. There we sensed that we had reached the outer edge of the high country and that beyond the nearby pass lay the Flathead Valley. None of us wanted to leave the bright, glittering, tingling high country. We basked on our backs amidst wild flowers. The sun burned our faces a deeper brown. Beyond that pass were cares and involvements. Up here was challenge and beauty and hardship. Up here was deep contentment and

250

peace. It seemed incredible that there are men who would like to blast open such places and reduce them to the commonplace of man's world.

Reluctantly we bridled our horses. We were going down. In this harsh, untamed country we had found something which deeply served our spiritual longings.

LINCOLN BACK COUNTRY

The Lincoln Back Country, also in Montana, has a quality and remoteness similar to the Mission Mountains. In the former it was drier; there was less snow, and although rugged in spots, much of it was smooth and rounded and more negotiable. We saw lots of flowers in both areas because of the late melting of the snow but in the Lincoln Back Country we saw more game or signs of game. On the tops we found many dusty spots which had been literally clawed into furrows by grizzlies. The marks were fresh, perhaps made on the morning of the day we saw them, since the claw marks in the dust were unpitted by rain.

As we walked over some of those open ridges, they reminded me a bit of timber line two thousand miles to the north along the Taylor Highway in the Yukon country. These mountains were not as aloof as that west rim of the Yukon. But there was a sense of expansiveness in traversing these ridges — as when I walked across the grassy plain of Thunderhead in the Smokies forty years ago. The rude outcrops of underlying rock were steep and rough but climbable. In the Missions there was rock that was not climbed. In the Lincoln country my mind said I could hike almost anywhere I willed.

From an unknown ridge we looked into a sweeping valley (Sourdough Valley) with bands of rock slicing across an

252

otherwise continuous but marginal evergreen forest. Tiny streams collected in small ravines. There were several modest lakes, in one of which we saw a dozen elk disporting themselves — galloping around and churning up the water. They were completely unaware of our presence. They were probably trying to get rid of flies, but their antics were so free and abandoned, one had the impression they were cavorting just for the fun of it. I would hate to have to deny that they were not enjoying the water. Here was another intimate glimpse of a substantial band of wild animals in a wild setting unmarked by man.

On the return we saw bear grass, lupine, deep-toned gentians, and the most colorful of paintbrush.

Our chief guide was Cecil Garland, a merchant and saw-filer in Lincoln, Montana. He loved this rugged country. Cecil was young and hated past destruction and plans for further ripping open this country. Once a forester himself, he was intolerant of poor forestry policies and practices.

23

CANYONLANDS NATIONAL PARK
UTAH
1965

WE WERE introduced to another ecological province in an unplanned trip down a free-running stretch of the Colorado River below Dinosaur National Monument and above Canyonlands National Park. We entered upon it near Cisco, Utah — an unpaved, rocky and ledgey semblance of a road which followed the Colorado for the most part all the way to Moab. The road had been quarried out from the ledges and detritus immediately above the river and its flood plain. Over its rocky ribbs we bounced, and through its dust and heat we bored. There was open plains country at first but soon we came to its gorge — respectable in itself although lacking the colossal depth of the Grand Canyon and the verticality of Canyonlands. There were gorgeous purple vistas down the canyon; volcanic plugs and walls protruded above flaring skirts of scree. There were fawn-colored sand bars along the banks of the river and

254

solid perpendicular cliffs of deep orange stone, with polished surfaces black with the varnish of the ages. There was heat so intense one seemed to wallow in it as he walked through it, and a dryness which seemed to suck at every pore of one's body. There were colossal turrets of yellow stone, deep gloomy side canyons, extruding walls which ran across the country like fences. Broken and eroding pinnacles were reduced to the realism of statuary.

Once we went up a side canyon of considerable size which widened out into a fair and pleasant valley. We climbed a crisscrossing road on the headwall at its upper end and found ourselves driving into the outposts of a substantial forest. I don't know how high we got — eight, ten thousand feet, perhaps. The air was cool and humid. Moisture and vitality returned to our bodies. Paintbrush, lupine, primroses burst into rainbows of color beside the road.

After a time we descended into the bright, blinding caldron of heat and raw color along the river and followed the granular, gritty surface of the road to a highway above Moab. We had pioneered a bit of desert country which was hardly moderated by the presence of the mighty and languorous Colorado.

Our trip of the morning and midafternoon was but a prelude to a twilight trip onto the royal plateaus of upper Canyonlands. Although we were high, growth was sparse and xerophytic. We threaded the neck of the "Island in the Sky" and drove to the breath-taking escarpments which commanded the middle plateau and tortured canyons of the middle park.

There was more bronze than purple in the fading light. Before us were wide flowing vistas in reds and buffs over the middle plateau, and seared grass and spottings of pines and junipers. It was a huge arresting site but not as convulsive as the sharp gash of the Grand Canyon. In the orange light of the sunset one of the overall views took on the rich nuances of a painting by one of the old masters.

We pulled ourselves away and dropped over the escarpment onto an angular scraping which had served as a road to venturesome uranium prospectors during the war. We bounced and zigzagged down this wall to the middle plateau where we took off on a dry dusty bumpy road which wound without reason, and seemingly without progress, over desiccated plains. We skirted the base of the escarpment which was now above us and the yawning edges of other canyons still below us. In a maze of twisting and turnings we suddenly breached a belt of cool air which clung to a tiny oasis of willows at the edge of the Colorado. We followed the river upstream to lights and industry and the level plain around Moab.

On the morrow we penetrated the vast area south and east of the Colorado and its juncture with the Green. We took another look down from a lesser escarpment where we were closer to the russet stony ribs of the plateau with its softer yellow. Here were found Indian remains, arches and gateways, chutes and vistas, incredible in color and form.

It was a dehydrated plain, vast in scope with unbelievable rocky heavings and protuberances. It was surrounded by escarpments and walls, and became a kind of stony desert entity which shimmered with heat and wild color. Rainfall was minimal. There were only a handful of seeps and flows, called springs. Indians had ventured in, lived for awhile, and found the going too rough. Perhaps the weather changed; perhaps their civilization simply dried up failing for lack of water. They left pictographs which featured ladders and shields and cliffs and animals, human prints six-toed and six-fingered. What did it all mean? How had they lived at all?

Blackened walls and roof of the cool cliff attested it as an earlier habitation. But all that had vanished, and the National Park Service, in that land of meager rainfall, had installed machinery and motors and supplies and gear under that cliff without the protection of walls.

We camped in Squaw Flat. There was a good gush of water at the head of a hollow a mile away. We were on a kind of level, sandy, desiccated meadow from which heaved and protruded round turrets. Floors and walls of rock were of fantastic formations and colors. I don't know why we pitched a tent, except that Ed Hilliard suggested it, and it did protect some of our things from blowing away in the incessant wind.

Before dark we took off on a promontory of rock which bisected the valley. It was clean and rough and rolling, and our boots gripped its raw surface with ease just as our spirits responded to its raw, colorful, rolling vastness which had no precedent in our experience. Once on the rock we could clamber and walk and climb and wander for miles without touching soil. An occasional fissure stuck like a sword back into the rocks, but we could go around them, clambering everywhere on raw stone. Some climbed onto rounded humps of rock and stretched out and slept. Others inched to the top of higher humps and moved about looking as tiny as fleas on the summits. Ed Hilliard and Ernest Griffith moved over to a forbidding wall which blocked our view to the west. They inched up its naked surface to a sway where they sat silhouetted against the pitiless sky.

Although clouds were lacking, there was enough dust in the air to turn it into an angry flaming pink which spread over the whole western sky. We turned back to camp. Low walls of red

258

sandstone to the south of us were turned into shimmering immensities of scarlet.

In the half light of a desert moon the wind blew and tore and flapped and popped our tent throughout the night. Sand and dust sifted through the air and into our duffle and clothing. It was a prelude to another day when we went back into the vast heartland of the Park around the Needles.

Routes, not roads, clambered over sheer rock. We lurched and rocked on switchbacks too tight for turning – forward down one rung, backward down the next. Some slopes were as steep as a ladder; others were as loose as scree. Only the Devils Chute was level; the rest consisted of ribs, detritus, and vast acreages of mother rock.

Every formation ever conceived glared in rufous reds under burnished cloudless skies. Niches, alcoves, statuettes, colossal statuary, thousand foot walls, tunnels, castles and serrations towered over every meadow. Lanes and avenues split every cliff. Chesler Park, a gem of a desert meadow, was surrounded by hot glowing walls.

We stood in a fissure between mighty red cliffs which hemmed us in, and gazed down in awe upon a sunken meadow cut with rudimentary canyons. Hot as it was, it was as intriguing a scene as I had ever witnessed. Ten or a dozen of us scrambled down crumbling walls to its level and skirted overhanging cliffs and the belaying traps of the little canyons, squeezing through a rift in living rock so tight we could feel the pressure on our ribs. We came to a bulging coralline wall at the head of the valley and watched fascinated while Bates Wilson inched up to a little bench from which he dropped a rope to the rest of us. We were going to thread the exit of a shimmering valley almost as remote as the moon – so isolated that two dozen white people,

259

perhaps, had ever ventured there before.

Above the first bench we climbed unprotected up bald, sand-papered slopes, dwarfed by battlements and beetling cliffs to a pass in the rock — the key to our escape — whence we looked down to an enclosed meadow with gravelly soil and a few trees. As we ventured out of the fantasy of rock onto the little valley we saw a movement among the trees. I could hardly believe my eyes — robins — their flaming breasts reflecting the ruddiness of the sandstone walls. We found an old wash which rolled and slithered under our feet, burst through another fantastic slice in the wall to find the other members of our party huddled in a mantle of shade awaiting our emergence.

A POSTSCRIPT

In the years which have elapsed since the various *Journal* entries were made, changes have occurred in the status of many of the areas.

In the case of Dinosaur National Monument (Chapter 5), after a battle extending through three Congresses, the Echo Park Dam was in 1956 removed from the legislation for the Upper Colorado River Project and a proviso adopted declaring it to be the intention of Congress that no dam or reservoir constructed under the authorization of the Act shall be within any national park or monument. It should be noted, however, that the Congress has ignored this "intention" with respect to the backflow of water from the Glen Canyon Dam into Rainbow Bridge National Monument.

The position of the Okefinokee Swamp (Chapter 1) has probably been strengthened by the listing of the Suwanee River, which rises in the Swamp, in the bill to establish a National Wild Rivers System. See Senate Bill 1446, 89th Congress; *Wild Rivers,* a joint report of the Department of Agriculture and the Department of the Interior, May 1965.

On the plus side, the segment of the Missouri River (Chapter 22) from Fort Peck Reservoir toward the town of Fort Benton has likewise been listed for study in the *Wild Rivers* bill. See *Proposed Lewis and Clark National Wilderness Waterway,* National Park Service, Omaha Regional Office, 1962.

Favorable to protection is the movement to establish a national park in the redwood groves (Chapter 21). See *The Redwoods*, Professional Report prepared by the National Park Service, September 15, 1964; *The Last Redwoods: A Vanishing Scenic Resource* (San Francisco; Sierra Club; 1963). Offsetting this gain are the plans of the California Division of Highways for a freeway through the Jedediah Smith State (redwood) Park.

On the minus side there is presently projected a dam on the White River in Colorado which would create a reservoir in the Flat Tops Primitive Area (Chapter 5). This proposal of a private power company comes at the very time that the Flat Tops are being studied for reclassification as a wilderness area pursuant to the Wilderness Act.

A new transmountain road across the Smokies has been recommended by a National Park Service study group.

Also on the minus side is the revival of the plan to construct the Sun Butte Dam which would back water far up the North Fork of the Sun River in the Bob Marshall Wilderness Area (Chapter 8). An alternative proposal for a dam on the main Sun River would back water up both the North and South Forks, requiring removal of 54,000 acres from the Bob Marshalls.

The Selway-Bitterroot Wilderness Area (Chapter 10) was established January 11, 1963. Although the wilderness so set aside included 1,239,840 acres, more than 446,000 acres were declassified as wilderness and excluded from the previously protected Primitive Area of 1,875,306 acres. Thus an acreage only slightly less than that in the entire Great Smoky Mountains National Park was removed from wilderness protection. The reduction of close to a half million acres is particularly shocking. In June 1961, less than two years earlier, the Forest Service had published a brochure, *Wilderness* (U. S. Department of Agriculture, Forest Service PA-459) stating that fourteen and a half million acres of wilderness "as wild and just as free as ever" are "held in trust . . . for the use, enjoyment, and spiritual enrichment of the American people . . . The Forest Service bears with pride its stewardship of these unique lands and has long been *dedicated to keeping them intact for this and future generations of Americans."* A map in the brochure showing the location of these areas bore the caption: "Here are the wilderness — the wild and primitive — lands of the National Forests. They are today as they were before our ancestors, as *they will be beyond our time and the time of our children."* The 446,000 acres now deleted from the Selway-Bitterroot were included in the fourteen and a half million acres extolled in the brochure only four years before.

In fairness to the Forest Service it should be said that reclassification of a few of the Primitive Areas has resulted in modest additions to the acreages under study.

The wilderness and conservation picture is changing from day to day. This postscript is not, nor could it be, exhaustive or absolute. Numerous additional areas are under discussion for inclusion in one of several categories of reservations. Some established areas, like the Grand Canyon and the Everglades National Parks, are in extreme danger — the first from Secretary-approved dams, and the second from diversion of the natural flow of water into the Park.

There are many contending forces and movements. The crucial point is not what the picture may be at any one moment, but what forces are at work and what the trends are.

The most chilling single factor is the population trend. The sharply increasing population will produce devastating pressures upon wilderness, and for that matter upon our national

263

well-being. If, as some predict, the population should double in the next forty years the demand for physical resources, including some now found in wilderness, will be voracious. On the other hand, urbanization, industrialization, and the inevitable pressures upon the individual for conformity, all of which are entangled with overcrowding, will themselves engender a demand for the kind of space and attributes found in wilderness.

A disquieting factor is the adherence of land-administering agencies to outworn policies which are themselves destructive of wilderness. A new road here, another dam there, meaningless predator control – the list is long. Parkinson's law that Government expands automatically to eat up all available income has been permitted to override ecological imperatives.

The industro-technological coalition is a massive influence. Used unwisely it is both a destroyer of the countryside and a rapacious consumer of resources. It has made possible for a few generations the maintenance of an unhealthily large population and the existence of the incredible urban complexes with which we are bedeviled.

But the industro-technological alliance and attendant ills are, in someone's trenchant phrase, but a speck in the hour-glass of time. Only human myopia, or arrogance, of cosmic proportions will permit this coalition to overwhelm the wild grandeur of the earth which has required millions of generations to bring to flower. Industry and technology are not ends in themselves. Their *raison d'etre* is to serve, not dominate, mankind.

There are evidences of revolt against this ascendancy. They are hard to pin down because the revolt is more spiritual than activist. The revolt involves some restoration, to be sure, some beautification. But it consists essentially of recognition and protection of the ancient forces which brought forth the earth and its creatures. Aldo Leopold called it ". . . a state of harmony between men and land." Within wilderness it involves freeing the land, its vegetation and creatures, to find their own destiny substantially untrammeled by man. Within society it involves bringing about a happier balance between mankind and natural resources.

There are evidences of this revolt — in the spontaneous surge of lay conservation effort, often at grass roots; in the trend to sound conservation emphasis in our newspapers and magazines; in the appearance of a brilliant array of books devoted to conservation and wilderness; in pronouncements of the President and of his aides; in the speeches and bills of our Congressmen; and occasionally, even, in the opinions of our courts. The revolt is seen in the openness with which population problems and controls are being aired, and indeed in the unrest on our campuses.

The winds of change are freshening. They bring hope, but not assurance yet, for a world in which the major forces of the earth may again be in balance.

AFTERWORD

Since 1965 when Harvey Broome wrote his postscript to this book, certain things foreseen by him have come to pass, while others happily have not.

Dinosaur National Monument remains unviolated by any dam or other engineering works of man. Rainbow Bridge National Monument is still unprotected from the threat of the backed-up waters of Glen Canyon reservoir, nowadays referred to as Lake Powell despite the provision which conservationists had enacted into law as part of the legislation for the Upper Colorado River Project. Debate continues as to whether a protective structure of some kind should be erected below the great natural arch to keep out the impounded water or whether a firm agreement, legislative or otherwise, should be reached to limit the maximum pool level of Glen Canyon reservoir so that no impounded water enters on the National Monument. Meanwhile, the Glen Canyon reservoir after nine years has not yet filled sufficiently for its dammed waters to reach the base of the Rainbow Bridge.

The wilderness of the great Okefinokee Swamp — nearly 400,000 acres in extent — remains as wild and free as ever. Efforts to place the Okefinokee in the National Wilderness

266

Preservation System have not borne fruit yet. Though bills to effect this purpose were introduced in the 91st Congress and again in the 92nd Congress, enactment of this legislation will probably depend on how effectively the public makes known to Congress its concern that this national treasure be given the protection of the Wilderness Act.

The Suwanee River, rising in the Okefinokee Swamp may yet become the first river added to the National Wild and Scenic Rivers System. Legislation for this is expected to be introduced in the 92nd Congress.

The stretch of the Missouri River between Fort Benton and Ryan Island continues to be studied by the Government for some sort of federally protected status in its existing free-flowing condition. One of the questions to be resolved is whether this segment of the Missouri River shall simply be made a part of the National Wild and Scenic Rivers System, with its narrow limits on the amount of adjacent land which may be preserved, or whether a special Missouri River Breaks National River shall be established under new and separate legislation giving protection to much larger land areas warranted by the historic and scenic values of the region.

A Redwoods National Park in California was indeed established by act of Congress in 1968 after a long and bitter fight.

The proposed dam on the White River in Colorado, which would back the stilled waters of the river into the Flat Tops Primitive Area, has not yet been constructed, and it is unlikely that any construction will occur until Congress determines whether the Flat Tops Primitive Area shall be placed in the National Wilderness System. If Congress so decides, it probably will mean the end of this dam project. On the other hand,

267

Congress can deny the protection of the Wilderness Act to this area or can so re-draw its boundaries that the waters of such a reservoir would not flood any portion of the wilderness area designated by the Congress. In the latter event this dam on the White River in Colorado could very well become a live issue again.

The proposal by the National Park Service to build another transmountain highway across the wilderness of the Great Smoky Mountains National Park has been defeated by the people. After blindly resisting for 5½ years the insistent demand of the people that this great eastern wilderness remain unviolated, the National Park Service in February 1971, withdrew its highway proposal. The Park Service recommended adoption of the citizens' concept of a Circle-the-Smokies Scenic Drive around but outside the Park. No proposed road project is ever fully dead and the continued vigilance of those who love the Great Smokies and all our national parks will be necessary to make sure it is never resurrected.

Both the north and the south forks of the Sun River in the Bob Marshall Wilderness in Montana continue to flow wild and free. The threat of one or the other of the Sun Butte Dams advocated by the Bureau of Reclamation may rise again, but the strength of the Wilderness Act is a mighty defense as long as we are prepared to fight to uphold it.

Much of the 446,000 acres deleted from the Selway-Bitterroot Wilderness prior to passage of the Wilderness Act in 1964 may yet be placed in the National Wilderness Preservation System. The removal of this wilderness acreage (which includes some 200,000 acres known as the McGruder Corridor or Upper Selway) by the Forest Service from its own administrative wilderness system preceded the National

Wilderness Preservation System established by the 1964 Wilderness Act. As the fight gets underway to extend the protection of the Wilderness Act to National Forest areas it is certain that a full-scale campaign will be mounted to place in the National Wilderness System all those portions of the declassified 446,000 acres which still meet the standards of wilderness prescribed in the Wilderness Act, i.e., have not yet been logged nor roaded.

The proposals to build new dams in the last stretch of the Grand Canyon have been soundly defeated. It now also appears that an adequate supply of unpolluted waters to the Everglades National Park is about to be assured. The Corps of Engineers was forced to change its policy of starving Everglades National Park of water; it is now required to permit a minimum annual flow of water into the Park through the Corps' engineering structures north of the Park. The proposal to build a huge jet port immediately north of the boundaries of the Park was defeated. Finally, it now appears likely that the Congress will authorize purchase by the federal government of Big Cypress Swamp, located north of the Park and from which source flows a major portion of the waters necessary to give life to the Park.

These victories for life, of man and of all living forms on this planet, did not come easily. They were fought for with persistence and with increasing skill. More and more human beings have come to realize that they must live in reasonable harmony with nature or man will perish from this earth. As increasing numbers of citizens have become aware of this basic truth, they have learned how to make their combined voices effectively heard by the decision-makers. Today our nation is seeking a new environmental path, charting new courses which will set the patterns for obtaining a renewed and improved environment. Persistent effort will be required by each of us to maintain the momentum and to accelerate the pace. We have learned that conservation victories can be won where there is the determination and the skill to make this a better world for man and for all living creatures.

Harmony between man and nature was the dream of Harvey Broome. This ideal, of which wilderness was the foundation, he held to tenaciously. He thought of wilderness as "islands in time." "And," he wrote in a 1948 essay, "the generations to come need them for the same breath-taking vistas into the past and into the future. May they remain for all time — islands in time and space, where living men can detach themselves from their civilization and walk into eternity."

Stewart M. Brandborg
Executive Director
The Wilderness Society
February, 1972

270

ACKNOWLEDGMENTS

Anne Broome, in addition to having a part in many of these trips, has shared the travail of bringing them to print. She made the first typescript of my longhand *Journals* and has typed two subsequent drafts. She has read each draft critically and has given full play to her penchant for accuracy and consistency. She has, as becomes a full partner in the undertaking, been both helpful and strict in her comments. All, I affectionately acknowledge.

Dr. Edward E. C. Clebsch, botanist, and Dr. Arthur C. Cole, entomologist, both at The University of Tennessee, furnished important information; and Stewart M. Brandborg and Clifton R. Merritt of The Wilderness Society staff, reviewed a portion of the manuscript and made suggestions for its improvement.

Chapters 1, 3, and 11 were first published in slightly different form in *The Living Wilderness,* Whole Numbers 6, 69, and 81; Chapter 5 appeared in an abridged version in *Nature Magazine,* 44:1, January 1951. I thank The Wilderness Society, and particularly Harry E. Radcliffe of American Nature Assocation for permission to reprint here.

H. B.